MW00813933

GREEK AND ROMAN MYTHOLOGY

BY
FRANK EDGAR, Ph.D.

SELECTED ART BY
SHERI LEIGH LEWIS

COPYRIGHT © 1994 Mark Twain Media, Inc.

Printing No. CD-1829

ISBN 1–58037–020–9

Mark Twain Media, Inc., Publishers
Distributed by Carson-Dellosa Publishing Company, Inc.

The purchase of this book entitles the buyer to reproduce the student pages for classroom use only. Other permissions may be obtained by writing Mark Twain Media, Inc., Publishers.

Permission for the use of selected artwork from *Costumes of the Greeks and Romans* by Thomas Hope was obtained from Dover Publications, Inc., New York.

All rights reserved. Printed in the United States of America.

TABLE OF CONTENTS

© Mark Twain Media, Inc., Publishers

What is a Myth?

When you look up at the sky, you see the sun, moon, clouds, meteors, comets, planets, and stars. You may recognize certain star patterns (called *constellations*) such as the Big Dipper and the Little Dipper (also called the Big Bear and the Little Bear). You might know the names of the nine planets: Mercury, Venus, Earth, Mars, Jupiter, Saturn, Uranus, Neptune, and Pluto. Did you know that many of the names of these heavenly bodies come from myths?

What are myths?

Myths are stories of a special kind. They are created to give values to persons, places, and things. Myths respond to our need for some kind of reassurance and meaning in the universe.

Myths are traditional tales of a particular people—Indians, Egyptians, Greeks, Romans, and others—and are especially connected with religious beliefs and rituals performed at public festivals. These rites were believed to invoke a type of magic that would aid the growth of crops and promote stability in the land. Out of these rituals came songs, poems, and stories which explained how people acquired basic things like simple speech, fire, grain, wine, oil, honey, agriculture, metal work, and other skills and arts.

A myth is an attempt to explain other things, as well, such as a certain custom or practice of a human society (like a religious rite), or a natural process, like the apparent daily motion of the sun across the skies. In their imaginations the Greeks of ancient times saw a man driving across the heavens in a chariot drawn by fiery horses. When evening came, he dipped into the western ocean, and while he slept he was carried back eastward along the earth's northern rim in a golden boat shaped like a bowl. Even today children might hear their parents say at sunset: "Now he's going down—now his feet, now his body, and now the top of his head." Sometimes it's fun—even for modern people—to give human characteristics to non-human objects.

Myths were passed down by storytellers from generation to generation.

© Mark Twain Media, Inc., Publishers

Myths are mixtures of morals, poetry, and history that were used to teach humans proper behavior. Mythical gods, the Higher Powers, with all their own shortcomings, had certain standards, rules, and expectations with regard to mortal men and women—they must show hospitality to strangers, and they must keep pride within reasonable bounds (in the eyes of the gods, excessive pride, or *hubris*, was the worst offense and deserved the worst punishment).

Myths, then, are stories about certain characters—gods, goddesses, men, and women—and especially heroes. The stories of their adventures, triumphs, tragedies, devotion, and vengeance provide a history of the beliefs of ancient people.

People of more modern times create myths and heroes, too. For example, George Washington was mythologized by Parson Weems in the story of the cherry tree—a story about an event that never actually happened but was used to illustrate a moral truth about young George's character. Stories are told about other famous Americans, such as Ben Franklin and Abraham Lincoln, making them larger than life and heroes in our minds. Still other American myths include the stories of Paul Bunyan, John Henry, and "The Little Engine That Could," who demonstrated that great things can be accomplished through self-confidence.

In the ancient myths, the gods are immortal—they can never die. They reach out and touch the lives of mortal humans who *must* die, even threatening and invading them at times. The relationships between gods and men are always dangerous, always at risk. But they are relationships which make the study of history and literature more interesting and—FUN!

Research and Discussion:

1. Observe the sky on a starry night. Find the Big Dipper (Big Bear). What is the Pole Star? How is it used for finding directions?

2. Observe the sun at sunset. Though it looks like it is "going down," what is the real explanation for this apparent movement?

3. Research the lives of Christopher Columbus, Ben Franklin, George Washington, Abraham Lincoln, and other "big names" in American history. What stories about their deeds show them to have been people of "mythic" qualities, legendary types?

Define:

myth	god	hero
goddess	mortal	morals
immortal	constellation	hubris

© Mark Twain Media, Inc., Publishers

Name_____ Date _____

What is a Myth?

1. Myths are stories created to give _____ to persons, places, and things.

2. Myths are tales from traditions of certain peoples and cultures, such as the _____,

the _____ , and the _____.

3. They are especially connected with_____ beliefs and rites.

4. These rites were thought to invoke a type of _____ , designed to help

_____ grow.

5. Myths explain how people acquired basic things like _____ , _____,

_____ , and _____ .

6. The sun seems to move. The Greeks explained this by seeing it as a golden chariot drawn by

fiery_____ .

7. Myths were used to teach humans proper_____.

8. The gods considered _____ , or excessive pride, to be the worst offense, deserving

the worst punishment.

9. People of modern times have created myths about such American heroes as _____

_____ , _____ , and _____ .

10. American myths also include the stories of _____

and_____ .

© Mark Twain Media, Inc., Publishers

The Great Gods: Olympians and Others

The Great Gods lived on Mount Olympus, an actual mountain, the highest in Greece, nearly ten thousand feet above the sea. In these stories, Olympus also sometimes seems to be a place much higher in the heavens.

There were twelve chief gods and goddesses and several lesser ones. When Greeks began settling in Italy, the Romans liked the Greek gods well enough to create their own myths about them, although they changed many of the names. Even at the height of the Roman Empire, the Roman gods were considered identical to their Greek counterparts.

Here are the names of the chief gods and goddesses:

GREEK NAME	ROMAN NAME	CHARACTERISTICS
Zeus [ZOOS]	**Jupiter** [JOO-pit-er] **Jove** [JOVE]	King of the gods. He is sometimes angry at the behavior of gods and people, but he can also be a gentle and caring ruler. He is particularly fond of beautiful women, regardless of whether they are goddesses or mortals.
Poseidon [poh-SIE-don]	**Neptune** [NEP-toon]	Zeus's brother. God of the ocean and of earthquakes. He is often distinguished in art by the fisherman's trident he carries—a three-pronged spear.
Hera [HEE-ruh]	**Juno** [JOO-noh]	Zeus's wife. Queen of the gods, guardian of marriage. She is a great lady and diplomat. Though she is often jealous and nags her husband, she can also be a tender and loving wife.
Athena [uh-THEEN-uh]	**Minerva** [min-ER-vuh]	Daughter of Zeus (born, it is said, from his brain, when he had a bad headache). She is the goddess of wisdom and war, patriotism and good citizenship. She is the protector and namesake for the city of Athens.
Apollo [uh-PAW-loh]	**Apollo**	Son of Zeus. God of poetry, music, and medicine, and god of light. He is associated with the sun.

© Mark Twain Media, Inc., Publishers

GREEK NAME	ROMAN NAME	CHARACTERISTICS
Artemis [AR-tem-is]	**Diana** [die-AN-uh]	Apollo's twin sister. Goddess of hunting and of wild things. She is associated with the moon. She is sometimes called "Cynthia."
Ares [AIR-eez]	**Mars** [MARZ]	Son of Zeus. Terrible god of war.
Hephaestus [hee-FES-tuhs]	**Vulcan** [VUL-kan]	Son of Zeus and Hera, the lame blacksmith god of fire.
Aphrodite [af-roh-DIE-tee]	**Venus** [VEE-nuhs]	The wife of Hephaestus, she is the goddess of love and beauty. She is said to have been born of the sea foam. Her son, **Eros** [AIR-ohss] (the Roman **Cupid** [KUE-pid]), shoots arrows which cause men and women to fall in love. Another son, Aeneas [ee-NEE-uhs], is a mortal man, considered to be the ancestor of the Romans.
Hermes [HER-meez]	**Mercury** [MER-cure-ee]	Son of Zeus. Messenger of the gods, he is also the god of science and invention.
Hestia [HES-tee-uh]	**Vesta** [VES-tuh]	Zeus's sister. Goddess of the hearth and home.
Demeter [dee-MEE-ter]	**Ceres** [SEER-eez]	Zeus's sister. She is the very important goddess of grain and agriculture. She is a kind of bond between heaven and earth.

These are the "Big Twelve," six gods and six goddesses, the top rank of the Olympians. Their traits and characters are as clear and human as those of mortal men and women.

Along with the twelve Olympians there were other important gods. Zeus's other brother, **Hades** [HAY-deez], more commonly known by his Roman name of **Pluto** [PLOO-toh], was lord of the dead and the underworld (also called "Hades") where the dead go. As we might expect, he was a dim, shadowy figure. There was also the great earth god **Pan**, god of woods and fields, who was half man (his upper part) and half goat (his lower part). Pan often played his "pipes," a kind of flute made from several tubes of reeds bound together. He was not often seen, but when he played on his pipes the woods were full of rather eerie music, which, especially at twilight, often scared people just to hear it, causing them to *panic*, as we say. The word *panic* comes from the name *Pan*.

Another important earth god was **Dionysus** [die-on-IS-uhs] (the Roman **Bacchus** [BAK-uhs]), god of wine and revelry, dancing and drama. Myths tell of his coming from faraway lands, bringing with him a new ecstatic (emotionally rapturous) religion and dancing followers of wild behavior, including the Maenads ("raving women"), satyrs (half goat, like Pan), and sileni (half horse). His opponents, defenders of more dignified old-time religions, despised his cult and fought it. But in the end, Dionysus was recognized as a god—perhaps the most popular of all gods.

There were several groups of minor divinities. Beautiful young women called **nymphs** guarded different parts of nature. Nymphs called Dryads lived in the woods, sometimes inside trees. Other nymphs called Nereids, daughters of Poseidon, lived in the sea.

The nine **Muses**, daughters of Zeus and Mnemosyne [nee-MOSS-in-ee] (Zeus had several wives), lived on the heights of Mounts Parnassus, Pindos, and Helicon, whose springs and streams were sacred to them, as were the palm tree and the laurel. Apollo, god of poetry and music, was naturally their patron and leader. They were goddesses of various arts, mostly literary. Terpsichore [terp-SIK-oh-ree] was Muse of choral song and dance, Euterpe [yoo-TER-pee] of lyric poetry, Erato [AIR-at-oh] of love poetry, Polyhymnia [paw-lee-HIM-nee-uh] of sacred poetry (hymns), Thalia [tha-LIE-uh] of comic drama, Calliope [kuh-LIE-oh-pee] of epic poetry, and Melpomene [mel-POM-eh-nee] of tragic drama. Urania [yoo-RAY-nee-uh] was Muse of astronomy, and Clio [KLIE-oh] was Muse of history. Poets in need of inspiration have called upon the aid of the Muses for centuries.

Three goddesses called the **Fates** controlled the destiny of every mortal person, man or woman. There was Clotho [KLO-tho], who spun the bright threads of youth; Lachesis [LAK-eh-sis], who wound them on her distaff or spindle, distributing and directing them along the course of each human destiny; and Atropos [AT-roh-pos], the eldest, somber symbol of death, who cut the threads with her sharp slender shears. The gods who lived on Mount Olympus had control over the world and nature, but it was the Three Fates who decided the length of human life. Even the gods could not interfere.

Mt. Olympus was the home of the great gods and goddesses.

The great gods and goddesses of Olympus

Research and Discussion:

1. Discuss which of the Greek gods are like people you know and why.

2. On an astronomical chart, find as many stars and planets as you can that are named for gods or goddesses. (Note: Be sure to look for both the Greek and Latin names.)

3. Find other examples of the use of the names of the gods and goddesses. For example: Mars candy bars, *The Poseidon Adventure*.

Identify:

The "Big Twelve"	The Fates
Pan	Maenads
The Muses	Nymphs
Dionysus (Bacchus)	Dryads
Satyrs	Nereids
Sileni	Hades (two meanings)

Define:

panic   cult   patron   ecstatic

Locate on a map:

Mount Olympus	Mount Parnassus
Mount Pindos	Mount Helicon

Name _____   Date _____

The Great Gods: Olympians and Others

Give both Greek and Latin (Roman) names.

1. King and father of the gods: _____

2. His wife, queen of gods: _____

3. Goddess of wisdom, war, and civic pride: _____

4. God of poetry, music, medicine, and light; associated with the sun: _____

5. His sister, goddess of hunting; associated with the moon: _____

6. The god who rules the sea; father of the Nereids: _____

7. God of war: _____

8. The blacksmith god of fire: _____

9. Goddess of love and beauty; born of sea foam: _____

10. Messenger of the gods: _____

11. Goddess of hearth and home: _____

12. Goddess of grain and agriculture: _____

© Mark Twain Media, Inc., Publishers

Name_____ Date_____

THE GREAT GODS CROSSWORD

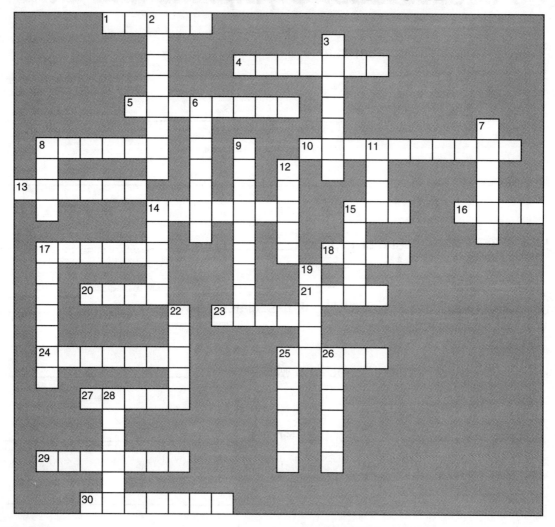

ACROSS

1. Roman archer-god, son of Love Goddess
4. Roman messenger of the gods
5. Greek name for god of wine and revelry
8. God of poetry, music, medicine, light
10. Lame Greek blacksmith god
13. Greek goddess of hearth and home
14. Roman name for goddess of wisdom and war, born from Zeus's brain
15. Earth god of woods and fields, half man and half goat
16. Roman god of war
17. Beautiful young goddesses of nature
18. Roman name of Zeus's wife
20. Greek king of the gods
21. Greek archer-god who causes men and women to fall in love
23. Roman love goddess, born of the sea foam
24. Greek goddess of grain and agriculture
25. Place where the dead go, and Greek name of the lord of the Underworld
27. Three goddesses who control mortal destiny
29. Greek name of Apollo's twin, goddess of hunting
30. Roman god of wine and revelry

DOWN

2. Greek name for the god of the ocean
3. Roman name for the king of the gods
6. Roman name for god who carries a fisherman's trident
7. Roman blacksmith god
8. Greek god of war
9. Greek goddess of love and beauty
11. Greek queen of the gods, guardian of marriage
12. Roman goddess of the hunt
14. Nine goddesses of the arts
15. Roman lord of the Underworld
17. Daughters of Poseidon
19. Roman goddess of the hearth and home
22. Roman goddess of grain and agriculture
25. Greek messenger of the gods
26. Nymphs of the woods
28. Greek goddess of wisdom and war; Greek capital is named for her

© Mark Twain Media, Inc., Publishers

10

Greek and Italian Geography

Greece is a land of capes and bays, peninsulas and islands, instead of being a solid mass like Spain or Italy. Pressed on the landward side by mountains, much of the population is located along the seacoasts.

There are several seas; the most important is the Aegean. It is strewn with countless islands, and trade and communications flow easily between them. The central island group, the Cyclades, extends near the coast of Asia to the east, facilitating trade and commerce between Greece and Asia. This makes the Aegean the true center of Greece.

Also important is the Gulf of Corinth and its isthmus (the narrow land bridge at the eastern end of the gulf which connects the two parts of Greece). Without this gulf, a lot of people would be land-locked mountaineers. It greatly increases the seaboard of Greece, and in ancient times this had a major effect upon trade routes and conditions of naval strategy and warfare.

Going west from the Gulf of Corinth and the Ionian Islands through the Ionian Sea, it is not far to the "heel" of Italy. The Greek lands—islands and mainland—are truly a series of bridges linking Asia with Europe.

Important, too, is the position of Greece in relation to North Africa. The north coast of Africa has played a significant part in the history of Europe. Europe and North Africa were once united by continuous bridges of land. This ancient continent, which has been named "Europa-Libya," was perhaps inhabited by peoples of the same ethnic group or race. When they were separated from each other perhaps twelve to fifteen thousand years ago at the time of the "Big Melt" (when the glaciers of the Ice Age melted and the seas rose, becoming one sea and drowning the land bridges), these peoples developed different life ways, languages, and cultures.

Greece is a land of small valleys ringed by mountains, such as those that form the eastern boundaries of Thessaly, including Mount Olympus, the highest (between nine and ten thousand feet) and the home of the gods. The Pindus Mountains divide Thessaly from Epiros in the northwest. There are also a few plains, and a few big rivers help to make contact easy within the mainland. Greece is particularly suited to be a land of separate communities, each one protected from its neighbors by barriers of hills or sea. In ancient times, each of these small communities had its own ruler.

Greece is not a fertile land. The soil is rich enough for barley, but not rich enough for wheat to grow widely. However, grapevines and olive trees grow abundantly, providing important products for trade with other nations.

Like Greece, Italy is a country whose history has been shaped by its geography. The country of Italy is shaped like a boot and is over five hundred miles long. The Appenine Mountains run all the way from the valley of the Po River in the north to Calabria, the "toe" of the boot, in the south. The Appenines are packed with volcanic rock and ash from volcanic eruptions. Though rainfall is fairly light, the soil is rich enough for the growing of wheat, grapes, and olives and the raising of sheep.

Italy's position at the midpoint of the Mediterranean Sea gives it a strong position in dominating that great sea in trade and military matters. Spain and Greece were cut off from the rest of Europe by rugged mountains, but the great plain of the Po River reaches well up toward the heart of Europe. The Alps, which border Italy on the north, have many passes giving easy access from south to north, so geography determined Italy's position not only in dominating the sea, but also in conquering southern Europe.

The Greeks were the main settlers in southern Italy and Sicily. The "toe" of the "boot" at one time was named Magna Graecia, or "Greater Greece." As different tribes moved around to the south and the west, the heel of the boot came to be known as Apulia and the toe as Calabria. These parts of Italy, along with Sicily, are very mountainous, and in some places the mountains come right down to the sea. Consequently, until recent times, most parts of these regions were cut off and isolated from the more advanced regions of Italy and are still poor in economic resources.

In addition to the Po River, which flows from the Alps in the north to the Adriatic Sea on the east coast, Italy has several other important waterways. The Tiber River begins in the Sabine hills and flows through the city of Rome. South of Genoa (birthplace of Christopher Columbus) is the valley of the Arno River, where lie the beautiful cities of Florence, Pisa, and Lucca.

The Adriatic Sea extends the entire length of Italy's east coast. The west coast of Italy, plus the islands of Sicily, Sardinia, and Corsica, surround the Tyrrhenian Sea. Most of Italy's good harbors and seaports are on the west side. Here the city of Naples, founded by the Greeks, was established long before Rome and was a major center of commerce. The capital city of Rome lies in the center of the west coast. From that position, beginning as a shepherds' village, it grew into a kingdom, then a republic, and then into a great empire—one of the greatest in world history.

Research and Discussion:

1. Study maps and globes; note the position of Greece and Italy in the world setting. What do you see as the most important facts about these countries' physical geography, regions, and cities? How do you think geography affected politics, government, diplomacy, and law? How do you suppose these countries were able to achieve such greatness?

2. Research the melting of the glaciers following the Ice Age. Report on how the landforms and features of Greece were made.

3. Research the volcanic activity of Italy. Report on the massive destruction caused by Mount Vesuvius in 79 A.D.

3. Ask a travel agent for some brochures about Greece and Italy. What are their climates like? What are the most popular tourist attractions?

Locate on a map (see pages 14-16):

Greece	Aegean Sea	Cyclades Islands
Gulf of Corinth	Ionian Isles	North Africa
Isthmus of Corinth	Ionian Sea	Athens
Mount Olympus	Pindus Mountains	Turkey
Italy	The "toe"	The "heel"
Appenine Mountains	Alps	Po River
Tiber River	Arno River	Adriatic Sea
Tyrrhenian Sea	Rome	Naples
Sicily	Sardinia	Corsica

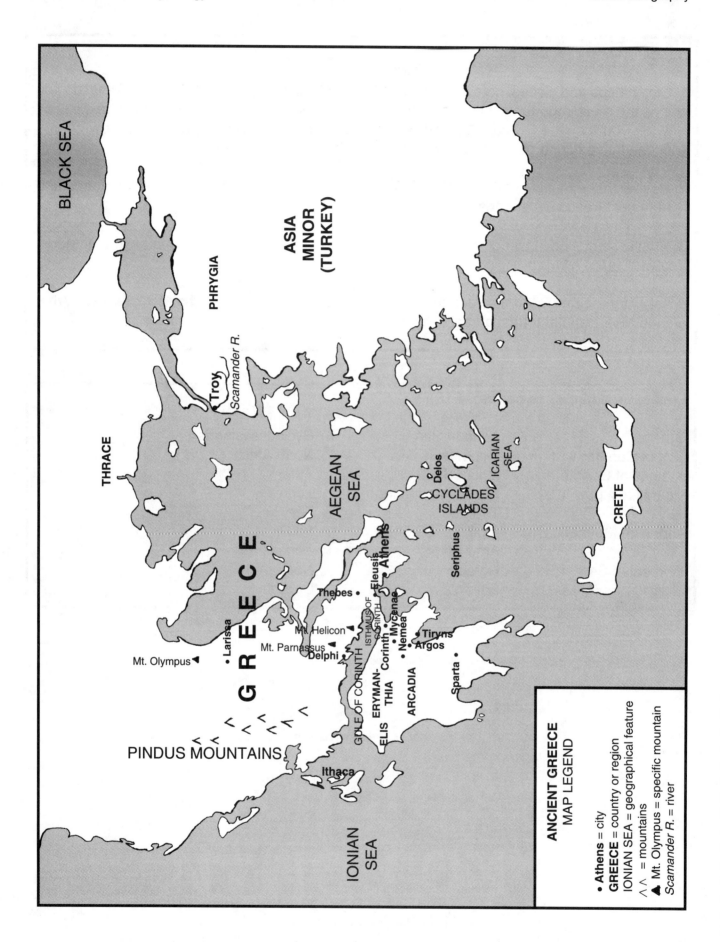

ALPS

Po R.

Arno R.

ITALY

ADRIATIC
SEA

CORSICA

Tiber R.

Rome ● Alba
Longa

APPENINE
MOUNTAINS

Naples

SARDINIA

TYRRHENIAN
SEA

SICILY Mt. Aetna

ITALY
MAP LEGEND

● **Rome** = city
ITALY = country
ALPS = geographical feature
▲ Mt. Aetna = specific mountain
ΛΛ = mountains
Po R. = river

© Mark Twain Media, Inc., Publishers

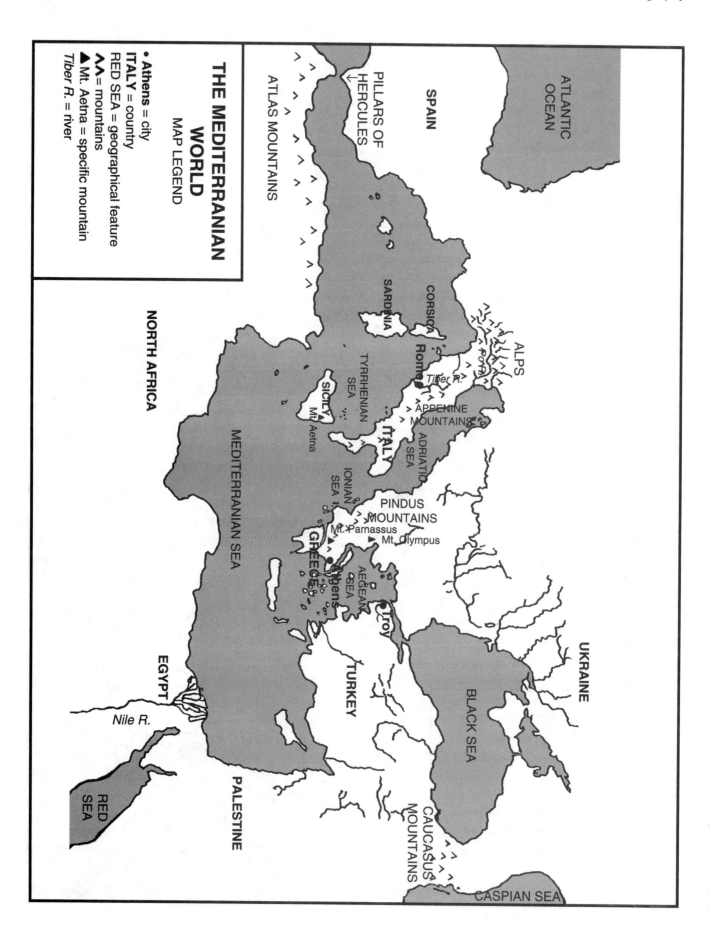

THE MEDITERRANEAN WORLD
MAP LEGEND

- **Athens** = city
- **ITALY** = country
- **RED SEA** = geographical feature
- ⋀⋀ = mountains
- ▲ Mt. Aetna = specific mountain
- *Tiber R.* = river

ATLANTIC OCEAN

SPAIN

PILLARS OF HERCULES

ATLAS MOUNTAINS

NORTH AFRICA

SARDINIA

CORSICA

Rome

Tiber R.

ALPS

PO R.

APPENNINE MOUNTAINS

ADRIATIC SEA

TYRRHENIAN SEA

SICILY

Mt. Aetna

ITALY

MEDITERRANEAN SEA

IONIAN SEA

PINDUS MOUNTAINS

Mt. Parnassus

Mt. Olympus

GREECE

Athens

AEGEAN SEA

Troy

TURKEY

UKRAINE

BLACK SEA

CAUCASUS MOUNTAINS

CASPIAN SEA

EGYPT

Nile R.

PALESTINE

RED SEA

© Mark Twain Media, Inc., Publishers

16

Name_____ Date _____

Greek and Italian Geography

1. Most important of the seas surrounding Greece is the _____ , the true center of Greece.

2. The main island group in this sea is the _____ .

3. The gulf that cuts Greece into two parts is the Gulf of_____ .

4. The highest mountain in Greece, home of the gods, is Mount _____ .

5. The geography of Greece creates a land of separate communities. In ancient times, each of these communities had its own _____ .

6. The three main crops that grow well in Greece are _____ , _____ , and _____ .

7. Pressed on the landward side by mountains, much of the population of Greece is located along the_____ .

8. The sea to the west of Italy is the_____ ; the sea to the east is the_____ .

9. The great river of northern Italy is the_____ .

10. The river that flows through the capital city of Rome is the _____ .

11. The western islands of Italy are _____ , _____ , and_____ .

12. The mountains that run the length of Italy are the _____ . The mountains that border Italy on the north are the _____ .

13. Italy's soil is rich enough to grow _____ , _____ , and_____ . Also, _____ are an important type of livestock raised here.

14. In Italy, the major center of commerce before Rome was the city of_____ .

© Mark Twain Media, Inc., Publishers

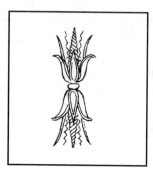

Creation

In the beginning, the universe was without form. It was just a vast hole, an abyss. This nothingness was called Chaos [KAY-ahs]. Out of Chaos were created Erebus [AIR-uh-bus] (Darkness) and Nox (Night). These two produced a gigantic egg, out of which was hatched a tremendous energy called Eros [AIR-ohss] (Love). Love created a goddess, Gaea [JEE-uh] (Earth), and a god, Uranus [YUR-an-uhs] (Heaven). Heaven and Earth were the first parents. Their children were a race of giants called Titans (or Elder Gods).

Cronus = Saturn

Uranus, first ruler of all things, proved to be very cruel and unjust. Finally his wife, Gaea, the Earth-Mother, helped one of their Titan children, Cronus [KRO-nuhs] to overthrow him. Cronus became king and married a Titaness named Rhea [REE-uh]. The rule of Cronus was called the Golden Age because all things on earth, including men (who had been fashioned by a Titan named Prometheus [pro-MEE-thee-uhs]), were living in harmony with the gods and with each other. The whole earth at this time was a paradise.

Zeus = Jupiter, Jove

Poseidon = Neptune

Hades = Pluto

But this Golden Age ended when one of the sons of Cronus, Zeus [ZOOS], overthrew his father with the help of Prometheus. Zeus made himself King of the Universe. He gave the sea to his brother Poseidon [poh-SIE-don] and the underworld to his brother Hades [HAY-deez]. After that the race of men declined morally from the Golden Age to the Silver Age. The Silver Age had some good things, too, but men had less respect for the gods and were absorbed by material pleasures. They continued to decline into the next Age, the Brazen (Bronze) Age. The Brazen period of constant violence and warfare did produce the heroes of the Trojan War. But as time went on this degenerated more into an Iron Age of poverty and misery, cold weather, crop shortages, and dwindling food supplies.

One version of the story of creation claims that the world became so wicked that Zeus saw he must sweep it clean of people and make a fresh start. He caused a great rain to fall (one of his titles was "Cloud-Compeller") and a great flood to cover the earth. When it passed, only a good man, Deucalion [doo-KAL-lee-on], and his good wife, Pyrrha [PEER-uh], were left. They and their children repopulated the earth.

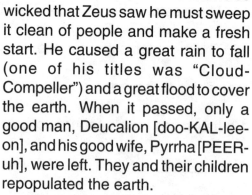

Zeus caused a great flood to wipe the world clean.

The authors of the Greek myths accepted a system of rewards and punishments. They believed that sin or wrong-doing—pride or greed or

© Mark Twain Media, Inc., Publishers

disobedience to the gods—were always punished. Sometimes the fault was in being too curious, as when the nymph Pandora [pan-DOOR-uh] disobeyed her husband and opened a mysterious box, setting free all the evils in the world. Most religions try to explain the origins of evil, and the ancient Greeks explained it with this myth.

But sometimes, it would seem, people were punished unjustly. The good Titan, Prometheus, known as the "savior" of mankind because he stole fire from heaven for the good of men against the command of Zeus, was punished by being bound to a rock.

For the most part, the gods lived their own lives apart from men, free of sickness and pain. And, of course, they never died. Only through a god's attachment to mortal persons could he know true suffering, as the drama of Prometheus shows.

Most of the time the gods lived happy lives, engaged in what we would call "trivial pursuits"—fun, feasting, and merrymaking. They even had their own special food, called *ambrosia,* and drink, called *nectar.*

The Greek gods had human traits and were fully capable of meanness, cruelty, and jealousy. Quarreling and feuding among the gods was fairly common. Most of them fell far short of perfection. But we must remember that the Greeks, unlike the Egyptians and the people of India, made their gods in their own image, in the image of nature, men, and women. Gods and natural objects were like people. A rushing stream was a lively young woman, a nymph, hurrying along to join her love, the sea. It is the humanity of the Greek myths that have given us some of the most beautiful stories the world has ever known.

Nymph

Beyond the Myth

1. Discuss the Four Ages of Mankind—the Golden, the Silver, the Bronze, the Iron. How are they like the medals won by Olympic athletes? What events can change a Golden Age, a happy time, into a Bronze or Iron Age, a confused and troubled time?

2. What is the meaning of the statement: "pride goes before a fall"?

Identify:

Chaos	Gaea	Eros	Golden Age	Iron Age
Rhea	Zeus	Poseidon	Silver Age	
Hades	Uranus	Cronus	Bronze Age	

Define:

abyss	nectar	ambrosia

© Mark Twain Media, Inc., Publishers

Name _____ Date _____

Creation

1. In the beginning, the nothingness was called _____.

2. The universe was without form, a big bottomless hole or _____.

3. Erebus and Nox produced a big _____ . Out of it came a gigantic force

called _____ .

4. From this tremendous energy were created Gaea and Uranus, also known as _____

and _____ .

5. From these two came the Elder Gods, giants called _____.

6. One of the sons of Gaea and Uranus, _____ , overthrew his father and became

king. His reign was called the _____ _____ .

7. This age ended when _____ overthrew his father, Cronus. It was followed by

the _____ , the _____ , and the _____ Ages.

8. When the world became too wicked, Zeus wiped out most of the people with a great

_____ .

9. The only people left were the good man _____ and his good wife_____ .

10. The gods were like men, but unlike men they never _____.

11. The special food of the gods was called _____ , and their drink was called

_____ .

12. The Greeks made their gods in their own _____ .

© Mark Twain Media, Inc., Publishers

20

Prometheus Gives Fire to Man

Prometheus [pro-MEE-thee-uhs] was the greatest of that race of giants, the Titans, descended from Gaea [JEE-uh], Earth Goddess, and Uranus [YUR-an-uhs], Sky God. To please Uranus, Prometheus created men out of clay (there were no women yet). He made these clay modelings look like gods, but he put into them bits and pieces of other creatures he had made already—the dog, the fox, the deer, the lion, the serpent, and the dove—so that this new creature, man, was a mixture of all these. These mixed traits were often at odds with each other, for courage might become rashness, caution might become timidity, and curiosity might be good or bad.

To balance out these different traits, men required education. So Prometheus, their father or big brother, so to speak, taught them many things. First of all, he taught them how to make crude tools and weapons out of stone and bone. But to go any further—beyond stone to the use of metals—he needed fire. Zeus [ZOOS] on his Olympian throne was the only one who had fire then, and he wanted to keep it for himself and his son, Hephaestus [hee-FES-tuhs], the blacksmith.

Zeus = Jupiter, Jove

Hephaestus = Vulcan

Zeus feared what men would do if they had fire. He had a low regard for them and really wanted to destroy them. There was always a chance of war between gods and men. Prometheus, the gentle giant, wanted to keep the peace, but as man's creator and benefactor, he knew his creature would never advance without fire. He decided he would steal a spark from the heavenly hearth on Olympus where the gods did their cooking. This he did secretly, catching a spark in the hollow of a fennel stalk (a plant used to flavor sauces), just walking out with it, as though it were a walking stick, and taking it down to earth.

Men's lives would never be the same again. Prometheus showed them how to make a hearth to hold the fire and then how to build huts around the hearth. So men began to come out of damp caves and dark holes in the ground and live in houses.

Then kind Prometheus taught them more: how to tame dogs, sheep,

Prometheus stole fire from Mt. Olympus to give to the race of men he created.

21

oxen, and horses, and how to plant seeds in the earth and raise crops—grains like wheat and rye and barley—to increase their food supply. He also taught them astronomy—all about the sun, moon, and stars—and how to gather plants and herbs for medicine to cure their ailments. Finally, he taught them how to write and how to figure arithmetic, which brought them very close to true civilization. But above all, he taught them how to live joyfully and with hope.

Zeus didn't like this. He had issued an order that the sacred element of fire should never be bestowed on mortals, and that any who disobeyed would be severely punished. Prometheus pleaded for the race of men, pointing out that the earth was getting colder, entering an Ice Age, and no longer radiating warmth as in the Age of Gold. Without fire, men would perish. But Zeus would not listen, and one day when he saw smoke rising from Arcadia in the heart of southern Greece, he knew that Prometheus had disobeyed. Outraged, he considered destroying the whole race of men, but on second thought he decided to punish the Titan alone. Prometheus, being a god, could not be killed, but he could still be made to suffer.

Zeus had two servants named Kratos [KRAY-tohs] (power, might) and Bia [BI-uh] (force). They were a pair of twin giants. He sent them to a forge in Mount Aetna (Sicily), the volcanic workshop of the blacksmith-god Hephaestus. The immortal blacksmith was compelled, much against his will, to forge the chain that would keep Prometheus bound.

Prometheus, whose name means "foresight" or "forethought", was well aware of his coming fate. He went to see his brother Epimetheus [ep-ee-MEE-thee-uhs] ("afterthought") and told him he was going on a long journey, which he had for some time foreseen and was prepared to accept, though he hated to leave beautiful Arcady. He told Epimetheus to take good care of himself. Then Prometheus gave him a large sealed box and told him to guard it well. He also warned him not to accept any gifts from Zeus, man's foe.

He then, without resistance, went with Kratos, Bia, and Hephaestus to his place of punishment—a high narrow valley of icy rocks in the rugged mountains of the Caucasus, west of the Caspian Sea. Nothing living had ever grown there since the world was made. It was a place of terrible lightnings, gusty winds, and whirling snow. Here Hephaestus, though he hated to do it—for he loved Prometheus for his goodness, as all the gods did, save Zeus alone—bound the Titan to a huge high rock and riveted the chains. Kratos and Bia taunted their victim, saying how with all his foresight he had failed to learn in time what it means to be

Zeus ordered Prometheus bound to a rock as punishment for stealing fire.

the friend of Man and the enemy of Zeus. Hephaestus, angry, told them to go away, which they did. He then told Prometheus exactly what was in store for him, how he would suffer from the heat and cold and terrible loneliness. And then Hephaestus sorrowfully limped away.

Prometheus, alone as no one has ever been alone since the creation of the world, had foreseen the price he'd have to pay for his generosity and kindness. He knew it wasn't really Zeus who was responsible for his suffering and pain. Zeus was only an agent of Fate, and Zeus in time must submit to Fate, too. Even the greatest gods have their limits.

And so Prometheus accepted his destiny and in this way achieved a kind of victory. He is, for all generations of readers, a legendary rebel against injustice.

Beyond the Myth

1. How does the Greek legend explain the different traits in human nature?

2. What are the different things people need to know to create a truly civilized culture?

3. Discuss other examples of how great people sometimes suffer for their good deeds. Cite some cases from history.

Identify:

Epimetheus	the blacksmith god
Prometheus	Kratos
Bia	

Define:

fennel   fate   benefactor

Locate on a map:

Arcadia (Arcady)	Mount Aetna
Caucasus Mountains	Sicily

© Mark Twain Media, Inc., Publishers

Name _____ Date _____

Prometheus Gives Fire to Man

1. The name "Prometheus" means _____ .

2. He was the greatest of the race of _____ .

3. To please his ancestor, Uranus the Sky God, Prometheus made men out of _____ .

4. He used parts of different animals, such as the _____ , the _____ , and the _____ .

5. Prometheus taught men how to make weapons out of _____ and _____ .

6. He taught them how to tame _____ , _____ , _____ , and _____ .

7. Against the will of Zeus, Prometheus stole fire from Olympus. He carried off the spark inside a stalk of _____ .

8. Prometheus pointed out to Zeus that man needed fire because the earth was getting _____ .

9. Zeus would not listen; he ordered Hephaestus, the _____ god at his forge in Mount_____ in Sicily, to make chains for Prometheus.

10. Prometheus went to see his brother, _____ , and left with him for safekeeping a sealed _____ .

11. Two servants of Zeus, Kratos, whose name means " _____ " and Bia, whose name means " _____ ", led Prometheus away to the _____ Mountains.

12. Prometheus, bound, knew that it wasn't just Zeus who was responsible for his sufferings. It was _____ .

How Evil Came Into the World

Although Zeus [ZOOS] had punished Prometheus [pro-MEE-thee-uhs] for giving fire to Man, he couldn't take the fire away from Man. The law of Olympus was that no god could take away any gift that another immortal had given. Zeus could only bestow another gift that might balance the account with Prometheus. So he called his son and chief craftsman, Hephaestus [hee-FES-tuhs], the blacksmith, and told him to make a new creature, like nothing known before—a creature made up of all good things, but also with their opposites.

Zeus = Jupiter, Jove

Hephaestus = Vulcan

So Hephaestus, who must have been the most industrious of all the gods, took a lump of clay and mixed into it a little bit of everything, from gold to gravel, from honey to gall, sweet things and bitter things and contradictory things: love and hate, kindness and cruelty, faithfulness and inconstancy, beauty and treachery, a little bit of heaven and a great deal of earth. He created a lovely creature—the first woman. (How men got along without women before that, only the gods knew!) The goddess Athena [uh-THEEN-uh] dressed her in beautiful clothes and taught her household crafts like spinning and sewing. Aphrodite [af-roh-DIE-tee], the Love Goddess, gave her beauty, of course, and the gift of sweet talk, but she also put all kinds of cunning tricks into her mind. All the gods gave her something, so they called her "Pandora" [pan-DOOR-uh], which means "All-Gifted."

Athena = Minerva

Aphrodite = Venus

Zeus directed that Hermes [HER-meez], the Messenger, take Pandora to Epimetheus [ep-ee-MEE-thee-uhs], brother of Prometheus, to be his wife. This was to show Epimetheus that the gods bore him no grudge or ill will because of his brother's rebellion.

Hermes = Mercury

Epimetheus—"Afterthought"—who never could foretell the consequences of his actions and often got into trouble without far-sighted Prometheus to guide him, naturally received the beautiful Pandora with great joy. He forgot his brother's warning about accepting gifts from Zeus. He was still guarding the sealed box that Prometheus had left with him, charging him never to open it. He was so charmed, however, with his new mate, Pandora, that he almost forgot the box until one day she

Pandora with the Forbidden Box

© Mark Twain Media, Inc., Publishers

25

asked what it was. Epimetheus, remembering his brother's warning, put her off. And so, for awhile, everything was fine.

But one day when Epimetheus was out gathering a bouquet for his beautiful bride, the too-curious Pandora broke the seal and lifted the lid of the box. Out flew big horseflies and wasps, beetles and bats, terrible creatures, stinging and poisonous—all the bad things that Prometheus, with careful foresight, had gathered together—sins and plagues and misery—and guarded so that the Golden Age and happiness of men might go on. And now they had all flown out into the world because of an undisciplined woman! Pandora was not a bad girl—just a little too curious about things better left alone.

However, one good thing remained in the box after the bad things had flown out and away. Hope, a beautiful, angelic little figure, had remained at the bottom of the box of evil things. Hope reassured Pandora and Epimetheus that she would never leave them. As we say, "While there's life, there's hope."

When Pandora opened the box, all the bad things that Prometheus had trapped inside flew out and escaped into the world.

Beyond the Myth

Why do you suppose the Greeks blamed the first woman for bringing evil into the world? Why not a man or a god?

Identify:

Pandora   Epimetheus

Define:

curiosity   hope

© Mark Twain Media, Inc., Publishers   26

Name_____   Date _____

How Evil Came Into the World

1. What was the law of Olympus, with regard to gifts of the gods?

_____

_____

2. In making the first woman, Hephaestus used opposite things, such as _____ and

_____ , _____ and _____ .

3. The goddess Athena gave Pandora lovely_____ and taught her household skills like

_____ and _____ .

4. The goddess Aphrodite gave her the gift of _____ _____ , but put all

kinds of _____ in her mind.

5. Because all the gods gave her something, she was called Pandora, which means

_____ .

6. Epimetheus was so happy with Pandora that he forgot about the_____ _____

his brother had left in his charge.

7. Epimetheus, whose name means _____ , could never fortell the

consequences of his actions.

8. Pandora was not a bad girl; she just had too much _____ .

9. What happened when Pandora opened the box? _____

_____

_____

10. The one good thing that was left, a promise for the future, was _____ .

How the Seasons Came

Far away from the bright world of the Olympians was the gloomy realm of the Underworld. Here everything was dim and misty. It was a strange, eerie land of underground lakes, black rocks, and dripping water which, mixing with rusty lime, formed strange crystal shapes on the roofs and walls of the caverns. To drive away the damp, Hades [HAY-deez], king of the Underworld, lit many fires, which caused the dark waters to shine in a spooky way but did not snap or crackle as fires on earth do.

However, beauty is "in the eye of the beholder," and Hades thought his dim, dank world far more beautiful than the upper earth with its grass, trees, and flowers.

Yet he fell in love with a daughter of the upper earth—the lovely Persephone [per-SEF-uh-nee]—the favorite daughter of Demeter [dee-MEET-er], the grain goddess.

Hades made occasional visits to the upper zone to inspect his temples, though the daylight hurt his eyes, and the smell of flowers made him dizzy. One day he was driving his chariot and four black horses through a part of Sicily where there had been an earthquake. He was relieved to find that none of the cracks in the soil were deep enough to reach his realm. He was about to go home to the Underworld when Eros [AIR-ohss], the mischievous archer-god of love, upset his plans, wounding him with one of those arrows that make the wounded one fall in love with the first person he sees.

Hades = Pluto

Persephone = Proserpina
Demeter = Ceres

Eros = Cupid

Hades had just loosened the reins to urge his horses on home when Persephone, her flame-colored hair streaming red-gold behind her, came dancing along across the flowery valley with half a dozen other nymphs. As she stooped to pick roses and irises, Hades, smitten by love's dart, swooped her up into his chariot. Persephone cried out in surprise and confusion, but the other nymphs had fled and no one else heard, except Mother Demeter, who was far off and had seen nothing. Hades, in a frenzy, struck the ground with his spear; the earth opened, and the chariot

Hades took Persephone to the Underworld with him.

© Mark Twain Media, Inc., Publishers

disappeared into the Underworld.

The echo of Persephone's cry still sounding in her heart, Demeter moved swiftly over mountains, rivers, and plains, seeking her child. She wore a long black cloak to conceal her brightness and true identity and would neither eat nor drink. After many days she came to Eleusis, a town not far from Athens. Hungry, thirsty, and exhausted, she sat down by a well. Here came the four fair daughters of Celeus [SEE-lee-uhs], lord of that place, running and jumping like young deer, to fill their pitchers. They took pity on the poor old woman, as they thought her to be, and led her to their home, where everyone treated her kindly.

Demeter continued to grieve for her lost Persephone. But when the little son of the house fell sick, she nursed him and restored him to health. The grateful family wanted her to stay with them always. Now she thought it time to reveal who she really was. Announcing herself as the grain goddess, mother of life, she commanded the people to build her a temple at Eleusis, and she would teach them religious rites that would give them hope and happiness forever.

The good people of Eleusis built the temple, and Demeter sat there as a priestess and gave them good counsel. But her grief was great, and she determined that she would allow nothing on earth to grow until she had her daughter back. It was a dreadful year. The weather was terrible; crops would not grow. The ox teams pulled the plows through parched, frozen soil in vain. Winter went on and on. It looked as though famine would destroy all of mankind.

Zeus [ZOOS] saw that the situation was very bad, so he sent one of his messengers, Iris [I-ris], down to the temple at Eleusis to request Demeter's presence at a meeting of the gods. But Demeter would not hear of it—she would never consent to revisit Olympus or let earth bear crops again until her daughter was returned to her.

Zeus = Jupiter, Jove

So Zeus sent his chief messenger, Hermes [HER-meez] of the winged sandals, to the Underworld. Hermes told Hades he had been sent to bring Persephone up again by Zeus's command. Her mother had sworn to destroy the whole human race by famine, leaving no one to honor the gods. Hades knew he must obey Zeus's order. But he made Persephone eat some pomegranate seeds before she left him. The Fates had ordained that whoever ate in the Underworld would have to stay there or come back soon.

Hermes = Mercury

Hades loved Persephone deeply; he could not give her up, but for the time he let her go to her mother. Hermes took the reins of the black horses that drew Hades' chariot and drove Persephone back to the upper world to the temple at Eleusis where her mother waited. The meeting between mother and daughter was glad and happy, but Demeter still grieved that Persephone had innocently eaten the pomegranate seeds and that this would draw her back to the Underworld.

So patient Zeus sent a third messenger, the greatest yet, Rhea

Hermes

© Mark Twain Media, Inc., Publishers   29

Demeter

[REE-uh], his revered mother and Demeter's too, oldest of the gods. Rhea pleaded with Demeter to show pity and mercy to mankind, to restore the earth and give life to men, which came only from her bounty. Demeter finally agreed to compromise. For a third of the year—four months—Persephone would go down to the Underworld to live with her husband, Hades. But for the rest of the year—spring, summer, and early autumn—she would live with her mother on the upper earth.

So it was decided. Rhea led her daughter, Demeter, and her granddaughter, Persephone, into the presence of Zeus, who honored Demeter and promised her all her rights. Demeter at last was satisfied.

In a flash the earth was transformed—the cold winds hurried away, trees blossomed, flowers of lovely hue burst from the ground, and the time of the singing birds returned.

Demeter, in her kindness and generous bounty, gave seed-wheat to the son of Celeus, whose life she had saved. She sent him over the earth to teach the best ways of plowing and planting. She did not neglect her temple at Eleusis. There she established a cult and a feast, and there the people celebrated with joy and hope. Demeter was always kind; they called her the "Good Goddess." She became the "divine mother of sorrows" and her daughter the "bright lady of the bright seasons," spring and summer, a goddess who went to live for a few dark months in the realm of the dead, but then returned to light and life again.

Beyond the Myth

1. "Beauty is in the eye of the beholder." What does this mean? Do you think it is true? Can a dark cave in its way be as beautiful as a forest, river, meadow, or mountain?

2. What is your favorite season—and why? Do all seasons have their special beauties?

3. You may sometimes eat a popular breakfast food named for the goddess in this story. What is it?

Identify:

Hades	Hermes	Rhea
Persephone	Iris	"The Good Goddess"

Define:

chariot   pomegranate

Locate on a map:

Sicily   Eleusis   Athens

© Mark Twain Media, Inc., Publishers

Name _____ Date _____

How the Seasons Came

1. Hades visited the upper earth sometimes, but did not like it because the _____

hut his _____ and the odor of the _____ made him _____ .

2. While Hades was riding in his chariot through the island of _____ , the archer-

god, _____ , wounded him lightly with an arrow of love.

3. In a love fever, Hades kidnapped _____ , daughter of _____ ,

goddess of the _____ . He took her down to the _____ .

4. Demeter, the grieving mother, wandered the earth and came to the town of _____ .

5. After saving the life of a small boy, son of the master of the land, _____ ,

Demeter revealed herself and told the people to build her a _____ .

6. Meanwhile, crops would not grow; it was feared _____ would destroy mankind.

7. Zeus sent three messengers: _____ , _____ , and

_____ .

8. Hades agreed to let Persephone go, but she would have to come back because she had eaten

_____ _____ .

9. Finally a compromise was reached: it was agreed that Persephone should spend part of the year

with _____ and the other part with _____ .

10. The earth bloomed again; Demeter gave the son of Celeus _____ - _____

to plant.

The Horses of the Sun

Saturn = Cronus

Jove = Zeus

Before Apollo [uh-PAW-loh] took over the sun, it was under the charge of Helius [HEE-lee-uhs], a Titan and nephew of old Saturn [SAT-urn]. He did a good job and never rebelled against Jove, so Jove let him alone.

Helius had a son, Phaethon [FAY-eh-thon], which means "shining" or "the shiner." One day as he was coming home from school, another boy asked him who his father was. Phaethon answered proudly, "My father is the Sun God, Helius, who drives the horses of the day and the golden chariot. He lights up earth and sky. I am his son."

The other boys jeered at him; they would not believe it. Phaethon ran home, crying out to his mother, Clymene [KLIM-eh-nee], what had happened. "Is Helius really my father?" he asked.

"He is indeed," Clymene answered, smiling. "Why not go to the land where the sun rises and find out for yourself?"

Phaethon decided to make the journey. He traveled far to the east, across rivers and over mountains, until he came to the palace of the sun, bathed in white light. Helius received him with joy and, as proof of his loving fatherhood, told the boy he would give him anything he wished.

"Oh my father," Phaethon replied, "let me drive the Horses of the Sun for just one day."

Helius was shocked and appalled. He realized how rash he had been in promising the boy anything. But he could not recall his promise—that was one of the eternal rules of the gods. All he could do was caution Phaethon and beg him to ask for something else. He warned the boy about the steepness of the way, both the ascent in the morning and the coming down in the evening. He warned him, too, about the monsters of the sky that lay in wait: the wild bull (Taurus), the giant crab with tearing claws (Cancer), the stinging scorpion (Scorpio), and the lion with huge jaws (Leo)—what we call the Signs of the Zodiac. "At times, Phaethon" he said, "the horses rear and plunge so that even I can't hold them! And you, after all, are only a boy."

But Phaethon was determined. All these dangers were only challenges for him. Sometimes children just won't listen.

So Helius sadly accepted what he could not call back. He led the way to the chariot of gold.

Eos [EE-ohs], the Dawn, flung open the silvery doors of the East with her pink fingers. They saw the stars fade and the moon hurry off, growing pale. The four horses, breathing fire, their hoofs gleaming with light, were led out from their stalls and harnessed to the shining chariot.

Helius gave Phaethon some last warnings. "Spare the whip, my boy, and follow the wheel tracks." He pointed out that the route did not lie straight through the skies, but rather in a slant, a wide curve, that avoided both the

Phaethon

© Mark Twain Media, Inc., Publishers

North Pole and the South Pole. "Don't go too high," he said, "or you'll burn the dwellings of the heavens—even Mount Olympus! But don't go too low, or you'll burn up the earth. Always keep to the middle way and follow the track!"

With joy Phaethon seized the reins, and the Horses of the Sun dashed off into a sky that was still the color of violets and roses. But now that changed to gold. Clouds fell away, and the sun rose.

Almost at once the four horses sensed that the driver behind them was not their master. They felt the lighter weight, the lighter touch on the reins. They began to move faster and faster. Leaving the main track, they dashed off toward the high stars. Phaethon could not hold them. In terror he saw the earth spread out below him and the sky monsters closing in on him. The Crab reached out its sharp claws, and the Lion opened its huge jaws to roar; the Scorpion pounced with its long stingers. Somehow he escaped them, but meanwhile the horses turned and headed downward. Now the earth was burning, cracking open. The mountains were the first to go—the Alps and the Appenines of Italy, Mount Ida of Troyland, Mount Athos of Thrace, the Caucasus. Grasslands burned into deserts and seas shrank; the Nereids dove down to the deepest parts of the sea.

It took a very powerful god to handle the Horses of the Sun.

With heaven and sea and earth threatening to sink into Chaos again, the Earth Mother raised a mighty prayer to Jove. She could no longer supply men with food, all life was threatened, the very gates of heaven were smoking, the clouds flamed. "Great Jove, deliver us!" she prayed. Jove heard, but he had already seen the disaster. Earth's highest mountains were ablaze—Parnassus and Helicon, where the Muses lived, and highest Olympus were all scorched. Fearing the end of all things soon, the whole work of Creation reversed, Jove hurled an enormous lightning bolt at the careening chariot, then rapidly shuffled the clouds and drenched the blazing earth with rain until the fires were put out.

The forked lightning fell true and ignited the chariot. Phaethon, still hanging on, fell like a streak of lightning, or a falling star, and plunged head first into the river Eridanus. Here the Naiads, nymphs of brooks, fountains, and springs, found him. Full of admiration for his courage and pity for his tragic fate, dying so young, they buried him and erected a tombstone paying homage to his bravery. He had failed in his too-ambitious enterprise, but he had shown greatness, even though his reach had exceeded his grasp. His sisters, the Heliades, came to mourn him and were turned into poplar trees, their tears forever falling from their leaves into the river, shining there like

Jove

golden drops of amber.

Helius, of course, was full of grief. He no longer wanted to drive the Horses of the Sun across the sky. But Jove insisted and gave him a new chariot. The horses had come back all right, once they had shaken Phaethon off with some help from the lightning bolt. They galloped away to their stables in the West, like any horses after a long day's work. So Helius reluctantly resumed his duties, until the younger Apollo was ready to take them over. Clearly, only a Titan or a High God could handle that job. For anyone else:

"Who drives the horses of the sun, Shall lord it but a day."

Or even less, as in the sad story of Phaethon.

Beyond the Myth

1. "Sometimes children just won't listen." Have you ever gotten into trouble because you did not heed someone's advice? Can you think of a modern example that can be compared with Phaethon and the sun chariot? What about a boy who wants to drive his father's car before he is of age?

2. Research the greenhouse effect and the changes in the ozone layer that surrounds the earth. How do these things change the effect of the sun on the earth? Compare the real problems the earth is facing with the story of Phaethon.

3. The story gives the names of several of the twelve signs of the zodiac. What are the others? What is the zodiac?

4. What is the meaning of the statement, "His reach had exceeded his grasp"?

Identify:

Helius	Taurus	Phaethon	Cancer
Clymene	Scorpio	Eos	Leo

Define:

zodiac   amber

Locate on a map:

Mount Parnassus

© Mark Twain Media, Inc., Publishers

Name _____ Date _____

The Horses of the Sun

1. Before Apollo took over the sun, it was under the charge of _____ .

2. The name Phaethon means " _____ ."

3. Phaethon's wish was to drive the _____ .

4. Eos was goddess of the _____ .

5. One of the monsters of the heavens was called the Bull, or _____ .

6. Another was called Cancer, or the _____ .

7. Another was called Leo, the _____ .

8. The one with a poisonous bite was _____ .

9. Helius's advice was to "keep to the _____ _____ and

follow the track."

10. On Phaethon's wild ride, it seemed as though all Creation might sink into _____

again.

11. Jove finally put an end to the ride by striking Phaethon with a _____

_____ .

12. His sisters, the Heliades, who came to mourn him, turned into _____

_____ , their tears shining like drops of _____ .

Glorious Apollo

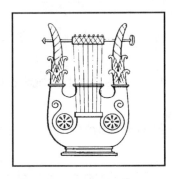

Zeus = Jupiter, Jove
Hera = Juno

Apollo = Apollo
Artemis = Diana

Leto [LEE-toh], a daughter of the Titans, was the kindest and gentlest of all the gods of Olympus. Her gentleness won her the love of Zeus [ZOOS], who made her one of his wives. This, of course, roused the jealousy of Hera [HEE-ruh], who drove Leto from Olympus. Zeus came to her aid and settled her at first on a small, rocky island, Delos, where Leto's twins, Apollo [uh-PAW-loh] and Artemis [AR-tem-is], were born. Zeus often came to visit them, bearing gifts. Later he led them over the sea to another land where they lived in a lovely garden with many good things to eat and enjoy. But when Zeus returned to Olympus, Hera came down in the form of a terrible beast and drove Leto from the garden. With her twins in her arms, she wandered off through wild, dark lands, hounded on by jealous Hera.

Fainting with weariness and thirst, she came to a pond of fresh water and stopped to drink. A group of country folk were there making baskets from the willows. These were ordinarily very nice people, but Hera had cast a spell over them, making them mean and cruel. They screamed at Leto to get away from "their" lake and be off somewhere else. If she didn't, they would hurt her. Leto pleaded her thirst, but they only laughed and jeered. Wading into the little lake, they stirred it up with sticks and their feet until it became muddy. Then they threatened to stone the poor lady.

Apollo was the god of music, poetry, and medicine, and he became the new Sun God when he replaced Helius.

Leto, holding her precious babies, stood tall, proud, and angry. "All right," said she, "if you love this mud pond so much, you can stay here forever." The heavens darkened as Zeus gathered the clouds; thunder growled. The people vanished, their clothes floating away. In their place appeared the green heads of frogs. Almighty Zeus still was protecting his beloved Leto.

He led her and her children back to a beautiful mountain on rugged Delos. Here Leto and the twins lived in peace and happiness. The children, nourished by ambrosia and nectar (the food and drink of the gods), grew strong and wise. Both learned archery, and Apollo also became devoted to music and poetry; he learned the art of playing the lyre. He saw his destiny as a prophet, proclaiming the word and will of Zeus to all men and enforcing the High God's decrees and

© Mark Twain Media, Inc., Publishers

36

laws.

Apollo became a great traveler. Before he was ten he made his first journey to the Hyperborean land, where spring lasted half the year and summer the other half. Over many years he saw many other places. He visited Olympus once, but the gods, other than Zeus, did not welcome him kindly. He was a newcomer, and no doubt Hera still hated him. So he wandered off again, looking for a place where he could build a temple of his own. He traveled sitting on a tripod—a three-legged stool with wings that skimmed over the water—with dolphins leaping and diving down around it.

In his search for sanctuary, he came to a great mountain called Parnassus, covered with snow. From the summit he saw a beautiful valley, guarded by rocks, with water flowing through the base of it and a rich plain at the end, thick with trees. Exploring this valley, he discovered a cave. First, Apollo defeated a monster like a giant serpent that stood guard over the place. Then, taking over the cave, he built his temple and below it a small room where one could sit quietly. He called the place Delphi.

Now he needed priests and servants for his temple. One day he saw a ship leaving from Crete. He knew the people of Crete were highly civilized with reverence for the gods and respect for law. They had guarded his father, Zeus, as an infant. They were people who could be trusted, Apollo thought.

In the form of a dolphin, fastest of all animals of the sea, Apollo sped to the Cretan ship and, with the help of Father Zeus who directed the winds, guided it into the Gulf of Corinth and the bay near Delphi. Back on land, in his usual form of a handsome young man, Apollo greeted the Cretans and told them of the great honor that was theirs in keeping the new temple as his priests, an honor they were bound to accept.

Apollo also found priestesses to help with the oracles. These women in turn sat on the three-legged seat (tripod) in the hidden room under the temple. There they grew inspired and muttered words that no one could understand, not even Apollo. But he found someone who could—the Great God Pan, the goat-footed, of Arcady. Pan taught Apollo the art of divining, and Apollo taught his priests so that they could find the meaning of the words of the priestesses and explain them to the people who came to worship from all over Greece. The Delphic oracle was to have a profound effect on the course of history. Everything that the priestesses said would happen came true.

Tripod

Apollo made frequent visits to his mother, Leto, and sister, Artemis, still living at Delos. One day he came to Delos riding over the waves in a new kind of chariot, with something like water skis instead of wheels, drawn by beautiful white swans. Zeus, who was watching from Olympus, saw Apollo removing the harness from the swans, and his heart swelled with pride. What a fine, strong, good-looking lad he was! His wanderings over sea and land had matured him, made him a man. He was about ready for higher things. It would soon be time for the old Sun God, Helius [HEE-lee-uhs], to

Apollo and the Horses of the Sun

retire, as he had been wanting to do since the death of his son, Phaethon [FAY-eh-thon]. Who better to replace him than this glorious archer-poet-musician-prophet-healer—Apollo. Zeus went to find another vehicle for his favorite son—instead of the flowery chariot drawn by swans, a chariot of gold drawn by the Horses of the Sun! The chariot had been forged by Hephaestus [hee-FES-tuhs]. Hyperion [hi-PEER-ee-on] had driven it first, then Helius, his son. Now Helius had earned his rest, and the fiery chariot would go to a new, younger driver, a new god of light.

One day just before dawn, Zeus summoned Apollo, now a man, and gave him his chariot and his charge. Helius taught him how to drive the beautiful horses across the sky. Afterwards, Apollo hastened back to Leto and Artemis and told them joyfully that the old spite of Hera that had forced his mother out of heaven had been more than redeemed by his new role as keeper of the Horses of the Sun.

Beyond the Myth

1. When the country people tried to drive Leto away from "their" lake, how was this a sign of hubris? Why, specifically, were they turned into frogs?

2. Have someone play the role of the Delphic oracle. Students should ask the "oracle" to predict upcoming events, such as: Who will win (or play in) the Super Bowl? When will it rain, snow, etc.? How old will the teacher be on his or her next birthday? Make up your own questions. Keep track of the "oracle's" predictions, and later check to see how accurate they were.

3. Research the use of psychics in modern detective work. How successful is this method? Do you think this is a realistic investigative tool?

Identify:

| Hyperborean | Pan | Delphic oracle |

Define:

| nectar | ambrosia | tripod |
| oracle | divining | sanctuary |

Locate on a map:

| Delos | Mount Parnassus | Delphi |
| Crete | Gulf of Corinth | Arcadia (Arcady) |

© Mark Twain Media, Inc., Publishers

Name_____ Date _____

Glorious Apollo

1. Apollo and Artemis were born on the island of_____ .

2. They were the twin children of_____ and _____ .

3. The food and drink of the gods arc called _____

and _____ .

4. When the country people wouldn't allow the mother to drink from their pond, they were

turned into _____ .

5. The fastest of all the sea animals, often accompanying Apollo, are the_____ .

6. Apollo became devoted to _____ and _____ .

7. Apollo's beautiful snow-covered mountain was called_____ .

8. The Voice of Prophecy speaking through the priestesses at Delphi was called the

_____ .

9. The priests for Apollo's temple were from _____ .

10. At first the only one who could understand the priestesses' words was the Great God

_____ .

11. Apollo rode in a water-chariot drawn by_____ .

12. Apollo replaced _____ as the new Sun God.

© Mark Twain Media, Inc., Publishers

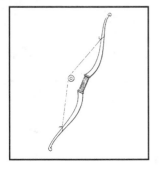

White Goddess of the Moon

Moonlore is a fascinating study. In the most ancient times, the Greek lands of the old matriarchal society were ruled by cults of moon priestesses. In those days, the moon had more authority than the sun.

At the time of the Creation, Uranus [YUR-an-uhs], Sky God, had given charge of the sun to his fourth son, Hyperion [hi-PEER-ee-on]. Hyperion married the lovely, radiant lady Thea [THEE-uh]. They had three children—Eos [EE-ohs], Helius [HEE-lee-uhs], and Selene [seh-LEE-nee]. They made Eos, with her rosy fingers, goddess of the dawn, put Helius in charge of the sun, and Selene of the moon.

Selene drove a silver chariot with two white horses over the night sky, as her brother Helius drove the golden chariot with the four fiery horses of the day. Her light was soft and silvery, but there was not enough of it to light up the sky every night; some nights were moonless.

Besides Selene, there were other goddesses of lesser light who were associated with the moon. Bendis [BEN-dis] of Thrace had a temple at Athens where little girls went when they were ten years old, dressed in brown tunics. If they didn't do this, they would never marry when they grew up. Another moon goddess was Hecate [HEK-at-ee], goddess of the night, who was in charge of funerals, but she also helped women give birth to babies.

Clearly, the moon had great influence on important phases of human life: birth, death, marriage, and little girls growing up.

Artemis = Diana

Aphrodite = Venus

No wonder ambitious Artemis [AR-tem-is] wanted to have charge of the moon. She was often ruthless and hard-hearted. She had little of the gentleness of her mother, Leto [LEE-toh], or the softness of Aphrodite [af-roh-DIE-tee], the Love Goddess. She had a mind like a steel trap. When she wanted something, she went for it. She was more than a match for gods and men.

As the great Huntress, she took over temples where animals were worshipped. She pushed out Britomartis [brit-oh-MAR-tis], who protected hunters, and Dictynna [dik-TEN-uh], goddess of nets, who protected fishermen. The revenues and gifts of their temples now came to her. She went after Bendis of Thrace and seized her temple, the one with the little girls, called the "Little She-Bears." No doubt she taught them all about hunting and how to avenge the insults of men.

Artemis began to take over Hecate's role, too, and so became the new Lady of

As the new moon goddess, Artemis drove the silvery horses and chariot of the moon.

© Mark Twain Media, Inc., Publishers

the Night.

Still, she was a little resentful that her twin had seen more of the world than she had. It wasn't fair! When Apollo [uh-PAW-loh] came home that night after his first ride with the Horses of the Sun, Artemis was quite proud of him but said, "Look, brother, you've traveled all over—to the Hyperboreans and everywhere—all those beautiful places. You traveled in that fancy chariot with the swans and the dolphins. Now our Father, Zeus [ZOOS], gives you the Horses of the Sun and nothing for me! It's not fair!" She went on to say that the next morning she would go with him to Mount Olympus. She would remind their father that she was his daughter, the new Sun God's twin. If Apollo had the chariot of Helius to light up the day, she must have the silvery fire of Selene to light the sky at night.

Apollo = Apollo

Zeus = Jupiter, Jove

Quite early the next morning the brother and sister rose up to Olympus. Zeus had not expected to see his lovely daughter; it had been a long time. But when he saw her, this white goddess, chaste and fair, he saw the logic of her request. What the brother could do in the day, the sister could do in the night. So he made the White Goddess the keeper of the silvery moon.

Artemis   **Apollo**

Beyond the Myth

1. What do you know about the moon? What influences and effects does it have? Do you know any superstitions about the moon, such as seeing it over your left shoulder (bad luck)? Do some research.

2. What does the relationship of Apollo and Artemis tell us about traditional brother-sister relationships? Was Artemis justified in feeling jealous of Apollo, or was she just a spoiled brat who got everything she wanted? Do men and boys still have more opportunities for achievement than women and girls?

Identify:

Moon priestesses	Hyperion	Thea
Helius	Selene	Hecate
Eos	Bendis of Thrace	

Define:

matriarchy   cult

Name_____   Date _____

White Goddess of the Moon

1. The moon priestesses ruled in the days of the ancient _____

society.

2. In the beginning, Uranus, Sky God, gave charge of the sun to his fourth son,

_____ .

3. The son married the radiant lady _____ .

4. Their three children were _____ (the dawn), _____ (the sun),

and _____ (the moon).

5. Selene drove a _____ chariot, drawn by two _____ .

6. Another (lesser) moon goddess was Bendis of Thrace. At her temple she instructed a troop of

ten-year-old girls dressed in _____ tunics. They were called the "_____

_____ _____ ."

7. Hecate, goddess of the _____ , helped women give birth to babies.

8. Artemis began to take over temples where _____ were worshipped.

9. Artemis was the daughter of _____ and _____ . Her twin

brother was _____ .

10. Zeus made the White Goddess the keeper of the _____ .

© Mark Twain Media, Inc., Publishers

Star Myth

One of the maidens who followed in the hunting train of Artemis [AR-tem-is] was the lovely Callisto [kal-LIST-oh]. She was as good as she was beautiful. The gods, including Zeus [ZOOS], loved her and showered gifts and blessings upon her. The greatest blessing of all was her little son, Arcas [AR-kuhs].

Artemis = Diana

Zeus = Jupiter, Jove

Zeus's visits and attentions to the charming nymph and her child naturally angered the ever-jealous Hera [HEE-ruh], who plotted revenge. One day she came down to the forest where mother and child were sleeping. When Callisto awoke, Hera touched her on the shoulder and changed her into a big, shaggy, brown bear. As Callisto's hands and feet changed to padded paws, she sank down and began to walk on all fours. Having accomplished this cruel trick, Hera went back to Olympus.

Hera = Juno

When the other nymphs came to visit Callisto, they found the big bear trying to pat the little boy, Arcas, as he slept. The nymphs thought the bear must have killed Callisto, so they drove her off with sticks and stones, though she looked back sadly at them. They took the boy to a good shepherd who became his foster father and treated him well.

But the bear kept coming back, prowling around the shepherd's hut, though he drove her away again and again at spear point. After awhile, the poor creature kept her distance, but continued to hang about at the edge of the forest. She seemed to be always waiting for a sight of little Arcas.

Callisto, in the form of a bear, tried to communicate with her son, Arcas.

As he grew, the boy drew nearer the forest, playing ball or gathering roots and plants. Sometimes the bear would amble out with a kind greeting in a soft bear growl. The frightened boy would yell loudly and run back to the hut.

As Arcas grew older, his foster father began to take him hunting and teach him the use of the spear. Callisto would always hide, though she yearned to greet her son again. One day, Arcas, with his spear, came to the forest alone. Callisto could no longer suppress her feelings of motherly love. Rising on her hind legs, she held out her paws in a loving gesture, trying to explain who she was and that she was under an enchantment. Arcas boldly raised his spear to kill the bear.

Hera

But something held back his arm so that he could not throw. It was Zeus, the All-Knowing, who saw beneath the bear's hairy hide and recognized Callisto. He took away the spear. Following the law of Olympus, he knew he could not undo what Hera had done. So he turned Arcas into a young bear, who understood at once what his mother had been trying to tell him.

Callisto and Arcas, now happily reunited, roamed through the forest glades together, free and content. But Zeus, to make up for Callisto's sufferings, had a far grander aim in view. He took them up into the sky. As the Big Bear and the Little Bear, they now had the whole heavenly realm to play in.

Hera, of course, was angrier than ever when she saw these new constellations, but there was nothing she could do about it. Zeus ruled the sky; his word and deed were law. All Hera could do, for what it was worth, was to persuade Poseidon [po-SIE-don] not to let the bears come down to rest at the horizon of the ocean like the other stars. They had to stay up there and move around the North Pole, always among the clouds. But Callisto and Arcas, after their long separation on earth, were perfectly happy as constellations, or star clusters, to be near each other in the high heavens, together again and forever.

Beyond the Myth

1. Do you suppose mother dogs, cats, horses, bears, etc., love their children as much as human mothers do and take care of them and protect them?

2. Observe the star clusters (constellations) of the Big Bear and the Little Bear (also called the Big Dipper and the Little Dipper). How many stars are there in each cluster? Which one is the Pole Star? How is it used for finding directions?

Identify:

Callisto   Arcas

Define:

constellation

© Mark Twain Media, Inc., Publishers

Name _____ Date _____

Star Myth

1. The name of the mother in this myth was _____ .

2. The name of the little son was _____ .

3. _____ 's attentions to them angered the goddess, _____ .

4. This jealous goddess turned Callisto into a _____ .

5. The other nymphs drove the big bear off because they thought it had killed_____ .

6. The nymphs took the boy to a good _____ who became his foster

father.

7. Arcas tried to kill the bear that came at him, but _____ held his arm back.

8. Since he could not undo what had been done, Zeus turned Arcas into a _____

too.

9. Later on he took Callisto and Arcas up into the skies and made them _____ .

10. Hera persuaded _____ not to let the bears rest.

11. Unlike the other stars, these two clusters had to stay up high and move around the North

_____ .

12. Some call them the "Bears," others call them the "_____ ."

© Mark Twain Media, Inc., Publishers

Love and the Soul

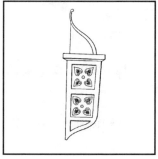

There was a king with three daughters. The first two were average looking, but the youngest, Psyche [SIE-kee], whose name means "the soul," was so beautiful that she rivaled Venus [VEE-nuhs], the Love Goddess. Men were so enchanted by Psyche's beauty that they left the temples of Venus to worship her, even though she was only a mortal.

Venus = Aphrodite

Venus, looking down at her temples, saw them neglected and deserted. Angry and jealous, she called upon her son, Cupid [KUE-pid], to wound Psyche with one of his golden arrows when she slept and arrange it so that the first man she would see and fall in love with would be the ugliest and meanest man in the world.

Cupid = Eros

Cupid, always willing to serve his mother, flew to the palace where Psyche was sleeping and lightly touched his arrow to her shoulder. Roused, Psyche woke up, but could not see him in the darkness. She was so beautiful that the Love God's heart skipped a beat, wild feelings rushed through him, and he felt weak. His hand shook, and he wounded himself with his own arrow. The Love God had fallen in love! He who had so often wounded others was now wounded himself.

Venus

When he flew back to Olympus and told his mother, Venus was furiously angry. She forbade him to see Psyche again and used all her arts and wiles to keep the girl's lovers and suitors away from her. Psyche's sisters were soon married, but no one wanted her. Men admired and respected her, but she was too good, too "high" for them.

Sorely troubled, Psyche's father consulted the Delphic oracle at Apollo's temple. The oracle declared that Psyche was fated to be the bride of a powerful monster who would meet her on a mountain top. When the dreaded time came, Psyche was dressed as for a funeral and left on the mountain alone. As she waited in fear and trembling, Zephyr, the West Wind, picked her up gently and bore her off to a beautiful valley of flowers. Here was a magnificent palace with golden columns. A gentle voice led her through spacious rooms, guided her to her bedroom, told her where to find fresh clothes and food. A table appeared with the choicest foods; invisible hands served her. Soft music played. She never saw the master of the palace. He came to her only by night and spoke softly and lovingly to her, not at all like a monster. She begged him to visit her during the day. He told her that if she saw his face, she might adore him or perhaps fear him and be in awe of him. He didn't want that. "I would rather you loved me as an equal than adored me as a god." Psyche didn't know that her invisible husband was really Cupid.

Psyche became lonely and begged her unseen lord that her sisters might visit her. Cupid feared and foresaw trouble, but he could not resist the

© Mark Twain Media, Inc., Publishers

wishes of his beloved. Zephyr brought the sisters down into the valley. At first they were friendly, but seeing the beauties of Psyche's palace, they soon grew envious and asked cruel, nagging questions about her husband. They were sure he was a terrible monster, or why wouldn't he let himself be seen? They urged her to take a lamp to where he lay asleep and see what he really was. Psyche, simple soul that she was, agreed. At midnight she lit the lamp and stole up to Cupid's couch where he slept. The lamplight showed no dragon, no monster, but the handsomest young man she had ever seen. She turned the lamp down, but a drop of oil fell on his shoulder, and he woke up. He looked at her with sorrow and reproach, and she felt ashamed. "Love can live only with trust," he said sadly as he flew away to Mount Olympus. The palace, gardens, the whole enchanted valley vanished. Psyche found herself again in her own country.

But she did not stay there. She wandered through the country, seeking her lord and lover. Finally Psyche came to the temple of Ceres [SEER-eez], where she pleased that goddess by helping the grain harvesters. Mother Ceres advised her to make up with Venus, whose son she loved,

Ceres = Demeter

to beg forgiveness and serve her. So Psyche wandered on to Venus's court on Mount Olympus and knelt down humbly before her, promising to serve her in any way if only she would be allowed to see Cupid again. Venus agreed but, still angry, was determined to make things as hard for her as she could.

The first chore was to sort out piles of different grains, all strewn together on the floor. The job had to be done by nightfall. Psyche knew that it was an impossible task. She sat on the floor, discouraged and hopeless. But Cupid still loved her, and he sent a whole army of ants to help out. They did the job in a matter of hours. When Venus

Ceres, the goddess of the grain, advised Psyche to make up with Venus.

returned that evening, she was angrier than ever that the task had been done. She knew Cupid had helped. She left poor Psyche with a crust of black bread, no praise, and no thanks. There would be more work tomorrow.

The next chore was to fetch a swatch of golden wool from a flock of sheep guarded by fierce rams that grazed on the far side of a nearby river. As Psyche approached, the river god spoke to her through the reeds. He told her to wait until later in the day when the sheep would be resting. So she waited until afternoon and then crossed through the shallows in safety. The rams and the rest of the flock were drowsing in the shade. They had

© Mark Twain Media, Inc., Publishers

left parts of their golden fleece clinging to the bushes. Psyche gathered them up and took them back to Venus. But all she got from her mother-in-law was another crust of bread and no praise. "Someone has helped you," said the furious Love Goddess.

The next task was even worse. It was to bring back a flask of black water from the source of the River Styx, high up on a rugged, rocky hill with steep walls, impossible to climb. Only a bird could reach it. This time Psyche was saved by an eagle who carried the flask in its beak.

But Venus would not yield. She decided next to send Psyche to the Underworld to ask Proserpina [proh-SER-pin-uh] to send back a bit of her beauty to repair what Venus had lost nursing her son, whom Psyche had burned with lamp oil.

Proserpina =
Persephone

Again Psyche felt despair. But again the friendly voice, so like Cupid's, spoke reassuringly with instructions on what to do. It warned her not to open the box containing Proserpina's beauty. With that advice, Psyche set out on her last labor. She walked downward through the dark caves and corridors of the Underworld until she came to the inner entrance guarded by the three-headed dog, Cerberus [SER-ber-uhs]. She spoke to him gently, caressingly. When she came up to him he was so charmed by

her sweet talk that he wagged his tail politely and lay down like any friendly dog on earth.

At the River Styx, Charon [KARE-on] took her hand, led her to his boat, and ferried her across. Psyche approached Proserpina's throne and explained her errand. The generous queen filled a golden box, and Psyche returned to upper earth as she had come. Once in the open air, she stopped to rest on a grassy hillside. Gazing at the little box, her curiosity, desire, and vanity were aroused. Why couldn't she take a bit of the beauty for herself? Then Cupid would find her even more lovely. So she opened the box—something with a strange fragrance floated out, and she fell asleep.

Cupid, of course, had been hovering around. He flew to the spot, gathered up the bits of beauty and put them back in the box. Then he woke her up and scolded her for putting herself in danger by disobeying him.

Cupid and Psyche asked Jupiter to make Psyche immortal.

Jupiter = Zeus

Cupid sent Psyche on to Venus to finish her errand. Meanwhile, he flew up to Mount Olympus and pleaded with Jupiter [JOO-pit-er] that

Psyche might be made immortal so that they could be together. Jupiter *Mercury = Hermes*
agreed. He sent Mercury [MER-cure-ee] to conduct Psyche to the Olympian
palace. They arrived in a blaze of light hiding Jupiter's throne, for a mortal
could not look on the ruler of the gods. Hebe [HEE-bee], the cupbearer,
brought Psyche a goblet of ambrosia. When she tasted it, all her woes and
weariness fell away. She was now not only refreshed but immortal—a
goddess—and more beautiful than ever. The mist rolled away from before
Jupiter's throne, and Psyche beheld the King of the Gods. She knelt down
humbly and thanked him for his gift.

Venus was now impelled to forgive Psyche and bless her marriage
with Cupid. Love and the Soul, after many doubts and trials, had finally
found each other.

Hebe, the Cupbearer to the Gods

Beyond the Myth

1. Discuss the statement, "Love is based on trust."

2. This story is, among other things, a cautionary tale about being too curious. Have you ever been
too curious? Has it gotten you into trouble? Explain.

Identify:

Cupid	Psyche
Venus	Proserpina

Define:

psychology

Name _____   Date _____

Love and the Soul

1. Psyche means the " _____ ."

2. The Love God is _____ .

3. The Love Goddess is _____ .

4. Zephyr is the name of the _____ _____ .

5. Psyche was tempted to satisfy her curiosity by her two jealous _____ .

6. Cupid woke up when a drop of _____ from the _____ fell on his shoulder.

7. "Love can only live with _____ ," Cupid said sadly as he flew away.

8. The first chore was to sort out piles of _____. Psyche was helped by

_____ .

9. The second chore was to fetch golden _____ , which she picked off the bushes.

10. The third chore was to fetch black water from the source of the _____River. She

was helped by an _____ .

11. The last chore was to go down to the Underworld and bring back a bit of the

_____ of Proserpina, the queen.

12. Finally, her husband brought Psyche to Olympus, and Jupiter, by having her eat ambrosia,

made her a _____ .

© Mark Twain Media, Inc., Publishers

King Midas and the Golden Touch

Silenus [sie-LEEN-uhs] was the oldest and merriest follower of Bacchus [BAK-uhs], the Wine God. One fine day he wandered off from Bacchus's band of revelers into a land called Phrygia, where roses grow. Drunk on wine and roses, the old man fell asleep near the palace of King Midas [MY-duhs]. The country folk found him snoring away behind a rose bush. As a joke, they crowned him with a wreath of roses and led him to Midas's court. The King of Phrygia was a well-meaning, good-natured man, though not too bright. He received Silenus kindly, entertained him lavishly, and gave him food and new clothes. Then he led him back to the jolly band of Bacchus, where he belonged.

Bacchus = Dionysus

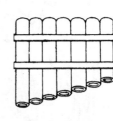

Pan's Pipes

Bacchus was so pleased to have merry Silenus back that he resolved to make Midas a gift. "You have been so good to my old teacher and companion," he said. "The gods don't forget. Ask for whatever you like, and you shall have it."

Midas, who wasn't much given to thought, didn't have to think twice or even once. He was already rich, but why not be richer? "I wish," he said, "that everything I touch might turn to gold." Bacchus looked at him strangely. "You shall have your wish," he said, and he then went off to listen to Pan's pipes.

Midas returned to his palace full of delight. He touched a marble column as he passed, and it turned yellow. He touched twigs and stones, and they turned to gold. But he began to have doubts when he stroked his favorite dog, and it froze into a cold, golden statue. The dinner gong sounded, and he hurried in to his meal, taking care not to touch his courtiers and servants. He was hungry. The table was loaded with good food—mutton and barley bread, goat cheese and pitted ripe olives. Grapes shone in beautiful colors—crimson, purple, and amber. Sitting down at the head of the table (his chair, of course, turned from ivory to gold), he plucked a luscious purple grape and popped it in his mouth. Oh horrors! It turned into a gold lump. In disgust he spat it out. He tried the soup—it turned to molten

Bacchus was the god of wine.

gold and burned his mouth. Likewise the bread, cheese—everything. He was stricken; at this rate he would starve to death. His courtiers, servants, and dinner guests were watching him curiously. Some of the more hard-hearted were trying not to laugh.

His little daughter Marigold, soft and sweet as an angel, ran up to him with compassion. "Oh dear father!" she cried, "Are you ill? What is the matter?" She embraced him lovingly, her warm arms around his neck. All at once she stiffened; her limbs grew hard. Her white linen tunic and peaches-and-cream complexion turned yellow. Her lovely hair did not change color—it had always shone like the rays of the rising sun. Little Marigold had turned into a golden statue!

Midas was appalled. He called out to the god: "Bacchus, divine Bacchus, come take away this terrible gift!" At first the god did not hear him. He was far away in the vineyards listening to Pan's music. But he heard at last and came to the king. "Well, Midas," said he, kindly, yet a little sternly. "Do you still think gold the finest thing in the world?"

"Never again, good Bacchus," replied the king humbly. "Take away this golden curse and give me my Marigold!"

What the gods give, they do not take back lightly. But Bacchus was too good-natured to pursue the punishment any further. Besides, he was still grateful to Midas for his kind treatment of Silenus. So he said, "Go to the River Pactolus and wash."

Midas did not hesitate. He ran out of his palace and plunged down the bank toward the river, everything his feet touched still turning to gold as he passed. He leaped into the river. As the waters washed over him, he felt born again, free of the curse of gold and of his greed for gold. He felt all his burdens drop away. His stiff golden tunic was soft white linen again; his belt and sandals were pliant leather once more. He had returned to the natural, the human. But the sandbars of the river where he washed away his sin turned gold and remained so always.

A new man, he ran back to his palace and embraced his daughter. At first she remained cold and hard to his touch. But in a few minutes she was no longer a statue but a warm, breathing, loving little girl, nestling in his arms.

King Midas was horrified when his touch turned his daughter into a golden statue.

"Oh, father, I had such a strange dream!"

"Never mind, my pet, it's all over now. Now let's eat—I'm starved to death!" He almost was.

The servants brought in more hot food, and Midas and his guests finished their meal. Never had food and drink tasted so good! When they had finished, Marigold took her father's hand and told him about some beautiful white flowers, anemones, she had found in the woods.

© Mark Twain Media, Inc., Publishers

"Won't you come see them with me?"
"Of course, my dear."
He walked with her to the flowery terraces of the green woods and found there greater joys than the gold bars and coins of his treasure house had ever offered.

King Midas and Marigold stopped to enjoy the beauty of the flowers, which they realized was more important than any golden treasure.

Beyond the Myth

1. What is the lesson (meaning) of the story of King Midas?

2. Did you ever know anyone who loved gold (or money or possessions) more than human beings? What kind of people are they?

Identify:

Silenus	Bacchus
Midas	Marigold

Define:

reveler	anemone

Locate on a map:
Phrygia

Name _____ Date _____

King Midas and the Golden Touch

1. The old teacher of Bacchus was _____ .

2. He wandered off into a land called _____ , whose king was Midas.

3. Midas wished that everything he touched would turn to _____ .

4. He first began to have doubts when he touched his _____ and it turned to gold.

5. At dinner, Midas was frustrated because all the _____ he touched turned to gold.

6. He was horrified when the same thing happened to his _____ ,

named _____ .

7. He cried out for the god to come save him, but Bacchus was away in the vineyards, listening to

the pipes of _____ .

8. Bacchus was too _____ - _____ to punish Midas further.

9. Bacchus finally came and told Midas to go to the _____ River and

_____ .

10. When Marigold was restored to humanity, she led her father out to the woods to admire the

beautiful white _____ .

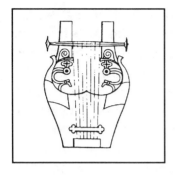

Narcissus and Echo

Narcissus [nar-SIS-is] was a handsome young man. He was so good-looking all the young girls who saw him wanted to be his, but he would have nothing to do with them. Even Echo [EK-oh], most beautiful of the nymphs, did not attract him, though she was desperately in love with him.

Diana = Artemis

Juno = Hera
Jove = Zeus

Echo was a follower and favorite of the Huntress, Diana [die-AN-uh], but even Diana could not protect her against the spite and malice of a more powerful goddess, Juno [JOO-noh]. Juno was involved in her usual activity of trying to find out what Jove was doing. She suspected he was interested in one of the nymphs, but she had no idea which. Juno went spying and looking. She encountered Echo and for a few minutes was amused and distracted by that beauty's happy, lively talk. Then, since she couldn't find anyone else to bully, she decided to punish Echo. The innocent girl's punishment was this: she was never to talk again except to repeat what someone else said to her. Juno told her she could use her tongue to speak the last word, but never to speak first. Of course, a lot of people would rather have the last word, but this was tough on Echo, who loved to chatter.

One day Narcissus was calling out to his friends, "Anyone here?" And Echo, under the spell of Juno, answered, "Here—here," happy because she thought the lad was calling to her. She was still hidden behind the trees so he couldn't see her. He shouted, "Come!," thinking it was one of his buddies, and of course she echoed, "Come!" and then stepped out with her arms lovingly extended to hug him. But he scorned her and turned aside. "No," he said, "I'm not going to let you take possession of me!" All she could say, appealingly, was "Take possession of me!" But by then he was gone. Poor Echo, ashamed and humiliated, wasting away until only her voice remained, hid herself in caves, where she can still be heard.

Juno

Narcissus went his own way, being loved by all the fair young girls and loving none. Perhaps he just wanted to be free, but he had to pay a price for it. Eventually, one of the girls he had rejected sent up a prayer to the gods: that he who could not love others should love only himself. Nemesis [NEM-uh-sis],

Narcissus was punished for being so self-centered by the goddess Nemesis.

Nemesis

the great goddess of righteous anger and justice, answered the prayer. As Narcissus leaned over a pool of water to drink, he was so taken with his own beautiful reflection that he gazed and gazed, transfixed, hypnotized as it were, by his own good looks, in a sense worshipping his own image. He knew now how others had suffered from his fatal charm. His punishment for his vanity was that he could never leave that image in the pool. Only death could free him from himself. And so it was. Never moving, he lay there until he died. His last words were to his reflected image, "Farewell—farewell." Echo, nearby, could do nothing to help him. All she could do was repeat his words, "farewell," saying goodbye to her beloved who had refused to be her lover.

It is said that when his shade (spirit) passed over the water that surrounds the realm of the dead, it leaned over Charon's [KARE-onz] boat to see itself for the last time reflected in the River Styx. Even in death, Narcissus could not forget himself. Nemesis had punished him, but he had learned nothing from the punishment. That was his sad fate.

But the lovely young maidens, the nymphs, whom he had rejected, were kind to him. They looked for his body to bury it, but could not find it. Where he had lain by the pool they found a beautiful new flower with bright colors and a strong but sweet fragrance. Still loving the youth who had caused them so much pain, they named the flower Narcissus.

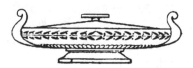

Beyond the Myth

1. What do we mean when we say that someone has a "fix" on himself or herself?

2. What does it mean to "have the last word"?

3. What is the scientific explanation for echoes?

Identify:

   Echo   Narcissus   Nemesis

Define:

   vanity   narcissistic

© Mark Twain Media, Inc., Publishers

Name _____ Date _____

Narcissus and Echo

1. Echo was the favorite nymph of the goddess _____ .

2. Echo was unfairly punished by _____ .

3. Echo could only speak the _____ word, never the _____ .

4. Someone who "falls in love with himself" is called _____ .

5. The repetition of a sound is an _____ .

6. Echo wasted away until only her voice, hidden in _____ , remained.

7. The goddess of righteous anger is _____ .

8. The punishment of Narcissus was that he was never to be free of _____ .

9. On his way to the Underworld, Narcissus leaned over Charon's boat to see his reflection in the

River _____ .

10. Where his body had lain, a beautiful new _____ was growing.

© Mark Twain Media, Inc., Publishers

The First Aviators

In the days of King Minos [MY-nohs] of Crete, the greatest architect, builder, and inventor was Daedalus [DED-uh-luhs], a man of Athens. Minos hired Daedalus to design the Labyrinth, a maze of winding passages, to house the terrible Minotaur [MIN-oh-tor]—half-man, half-bull—a kind of monster-god who every year demanded sacrifices of beautiful young men and women, many of them from Athens.

One year a hero appeared among the victims. This was Theseus [THEE-see-uhs], who was determined to kill the monster before the human sacrifice. But once he got into the Labyrinth, how could he find his way out again? His one hope was the king's daughter, Ariadne [air-ee-AD-nee], who had fallen in love with Theseus. Ariadne appealed to Daedalus for help. He provided a ball of thread, which was conveyed to Theseus by Ariadne's nurse, along with instructions on how to fix it in the wall and unwind it behind him on the way in. If he managed to kill the monster, he was to follow the trail of thread out of the maze. Theseus entered the Labyrinth, killed the monster, and escaped with Ariadne to his ship and away from Crete.

But Daedalus was left to face the consequences. Minos was not long in finding out what had happened and who it was that had dared to thwart his will. In a rage, he had Daedalus and his son, Icarus [ICK-uh-ruhs], shut up in a tower over the Labyrinth. There they could watch the sea and the birds, but had no hope of escape. Daedalus, the inventor, however, managed to occupy himself very well, tinkering and puttering and inventing new things, which he was allowed to do, for such things were useful to Minos. Daedalus had already invented a saw, and he could easily cut through the bars of his tower prison. But the main obstacles for him and Icarus were the height of the tower and the winding lanes and aisles of the Labyrinth below.

Icarus didn't listen to his father and flew too close to the sun. The heat melted the wax holding his wings together.

Then one day, watching the birds, he had a thought. Wings. He started asking for new materials—stout reeds of the kind Pan used for his pipes, wax, and the feathers of eagles. With the reeds he built a frame and waxed the feathers to it. He made a large set for himself and a smaller set for Icarus. When the time came, they flew away from the tower of the Labyrinth.

© Mark Twain Media, Inc., Publishers

For awhile they hid out in remote parts of Crete, strolling along the beaches now and then, improving their wings, still studying the flights of birds. But Minos was looking for them, watching all the ships, searching everywhere. So they decided to leave Crete and fly off somewhere else, perhaps to Delos, island of Apollo [uh-PAW-loh], who protects inventors and artists. Before they took off, Daedalus warned his son, "Don't fly too high or the sun will melt the wax and your wings will fall off. But don't fly too low or the waves will moisten the wax. Keep to the middle altitudes and follow me."

Apollo = Apollo

At first Icarus was obedient and followed his father on the straight middle course. But after awhile he got excited and began trying stunts. First he would drift down toward the sea until his sandals were almost touching the waves; then he would soar up, up toward the sun—higher, higher.

Suddenly there were feathers floating around him, a cloud of feathers so thick he could hardly see. In terror he knew that the sun had melted the wax; he was losing his wings. Down he fell, down, down, down. Desperately he tried to rise, but it was no use. Turning and twisting, with a last despairing cry, he plunged into the winey-colored waves of the deep sea, that part of the Aegean that lies between Crete and Delos, ever since called the Icarian Sea.

Daedalus, hearing his son's cry, turned back and circled the waters, but saw nothing except a handful of floating white feathers. Sadly he traveled on to friendly Delos where he, the master architect, built a temple to Apollo. Here he hung up his wings in homage to the god. He never again tried to fly.

Apollo

Beyond the Myth

1. Research and report on Leonardo da Vinci's experiments with human flight. Were any of his inventions similar to Daedalus's wings?

2. How is the story of Icarus like the story of Phaethon?

Identify:

Theseus	Minos	Daedalus
Ariadne	Minotaur	Icarus

Define:

labyrinth   architect

Locate on a map:

Crete	Delos	Icarian Sea

© Mark Twain Media, Inc., Publishers

Name _____ Date _____

The First Aviators

1. Daedalus was the greatest _____ , _____ , and

_____ .

2. King _____ of Crete hired Daedalus to build the winding _____ .

3. Daedalus helped _____ of Athens and the king's daughter, _____ ,

escape.

4. When Theseus killed the Minotaur, he followed a trail of _____ to find his way

out of the maze.

5. Locked in the tower, Daedalus began to study the flights of _____ .

6. When he started to make the wings, he used these materials for his purpose:

_____ , _____ , and _____ .

7. When they first escaped, Daedalus and Icarus hid out in remote parts of _____ .

8. Icarus disobeyed his father. The _____ melted the wax, and the _____

fell from his wings.

9. The place where he fell into the water is still called the _____ Sea.

10. Daedalus flew on to Delos and built a temple to _____ , who helps inventors.

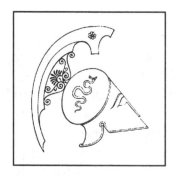

The Youth of Hercules*

Hercules [HER-kue-leez] was the greatest hero of Greece. He was, in fact, a demigod by birth (the child of a god and a mortal). His father was Zeus [ZOOS], and his mother was Alcmene [alk-MEEN-ee], a princess of Thebes. He grew up in the royal palace. When only a baby he showed his uncommon strength. Already he had an enemy, Hera [HEE-ruh], who was always resentful and jealous. The queen of the gods sent two big snakes after the child as he lay in his little bed. Hercules, who was not even two years old, woke up just in time. With his tough little hands he grabbed each serpent by the neck and strangled them. The royal household, which had heard the commotion, came rushing in. They were astonished. Clearly, this child was someone special. The prophet, Teiresias [tie-REE-see-uhs], predicted great things for him.

As Hercules grew, he received the finest education, though he was a slow learner and not very bright. The best masters taught him boxing, wrestling, and archery. He learned how to read and write—not common in those days even for princes—and all about music, both singing and playing. He learned horsemanship and how to drive a chariot. And as he grew older he learned battle tactics and the use of weapons and how to lead men in war.

One day when he was eighteen, he was walking along the road and saw two women approaching, one behind the other. The first one ran ahead to reach him first. He could see that she was tall and attractive, with painted cheeks and lips. She said, in a sweet, caressing voice, "Young man, you look like you don't know where you're going or what you're up to. Come see me sometime. I'll be good to you and show you a pleasant life. You won't have to work very hard, and you'll always have a good time."

Hercules asked, "Who are you?" She replied her name was Pleasure, but people who disapproved of her

Hercules = Heracles(Gk)

Zeus = Jupiter, Jove

Hera = Juno

The jealous goddess Hera made life difficult for Hercules.

*Although these stories about Hercules are mostly from Greek sources, the Roman name, Hercules, is used here because it is more familiar to most people.

© Mark Twain Media, Inc., Publishers

called her Vice.

Then the second woman came up. She was completely different, tall and beautiful, too, but with no rouge or lipstick. She was dressed modestly and simply in white. She had an air of nobility and truth. She spoke courteously but with dignified firmness: "I know of you, my dear sir. You come of a good family and many good things have been said about great deeds you might do. I'm not going to deceive you, just tell you the truth. Good things, the greatest things, don't come easily. They come through work and suffering and hardship. If you want to raise crops, you have to plow the land, sow seeds, fight weeds, reap the harvest, and toil in the sweat of your brow. If you want a strong body, you have to train it and make it serve your mind. You mustn't fear work and sweat. You must offer prayers to the gods if you need their help; you must humbly atone for your faults. You must love your country and fight for it. Men were born to pray and work hard. If you can learn these truths and apply them in your life and experience, you can become great and happy in the best way." Hercules, meek and bashful, asked her name. She replied, "It is Virtue."

At this point Pleasure tried to distract him, but Virtue won. Hercules made a resolution to follow the hard way, wherever it led. He would pay the price for that choice, but he would have his reward.

But it would be a long, hard fight for the hero. First of all, he had to conquer himself—his own unruly temper. One day he was having a music lesson. His teacher scolded him for carelessness and tried to punish him. Hercules, in a rage, lifted his lute and smashed it over the teacher's head, killing him. Of course, Hercules had never intended this; he simply wasn't aware of his own strength. But now he was considered dangerous. He was banished to the hills to live with rough herdsmen and toil and sweat among the sheep and cattle.

Hercules used his bare hands to kill the lion that had been threatening the countryside.

In those hills lived a lion who had caused the herdsmen much trouble by prowling about the flocks and herds and, now and then, killing the stock. Hercules went after the beast and killed it with his bare hands; he was a master of the stranglehold, as he had proved years before with the serpents. When he came back carrying the great beast, he won the respect and even the love of the herdsmen. That was the beginning of his rehabilitation, though he would continue to slip and stumble from time to time.

Eventually, Hercules married a princess, Megara [MEG-uh-ruh], and they had two sons. But Hera still could not forgive him for being the son

© Mark Twain Media, Inc., Publishers

of her husband and another woman; her malice always pursued him. So she caused something terrible to happen. The cruel goddess drove him temporarily mad. In this fit of insanity he went wild and killed Megara and his two sons. When he recovered his wits he could not understand what had happened. Filled with remorse, he sought atonement, if there was atonement for such a dreadful thing. The Delphi oracle told him he must leave Thebes and go to the south of Greece and serve the King of Mycenae, Eurystheus [yur-EES-thee-uhs].

On his way south he stopped at Athens. His friend, the good Theseus [THEE-see-uhs], welcomed him and tried to help him. He tried to point out that a mad man is not responsible for his acts, that some jealous god was behind the terrible deed. But poor Hercules could not reason things out that way. He knew he had done wrong, that he must be punished and undergo a long penance. That was why he accepted the Twelve Labors imposed on him by the King of Mycenae.

Beyond the Myth

1. Compare the two women that Hercules met. Is it possible to work hard and serve but have fun and enjoy life too?

2. Hercules was apparently not very good at schoolwork, but he was physically very strong. Do you think strength might be a type of intelligence? Are there other kinds of intelligence besides the traditional reading and math skills? Does a person have to be "book smart" to be highly skilled at something?

Identify:

Hercules	Teiresias	Alcmena
Eurystheus	Megara	

Define:

demigod	prophet	virtue
vice	malice	

Locate on a map:

Thebes	Athens	Mycenae

Name _____ Date _____

The Youth of Hercules

1. The mother of Hercules was _____ . His father was _____ .

2. The child of a god and a mortal is called a _____ .

3. He grew up in the city of _____ .

4. Teiresias, the Theban _____ , had predicted great things for him.

5. When he was a baby, he killed two _____ ; his first exploit when he grew up was to kill

a _____ .

6. The two women whom Hercules met on the road were named _____ ,

or _____ , and _____ .

7. Hercules decided to follow the way described by the lady named _____ .

8. Hercules was banished to the hills because he killed _____ .

9. His wife's name was _____ .

10. He killed his wife and sons because of a spell cast over him by the cruel goddess,

_____ .

11. The _____ told Hercules he must serve the King of Mycenae

to atone for his crime.

12. The King of Mycenae ordered him to perform _____ _____

as punishment.

© Mark Twain Media, Inc., Publishers

The Twelve Labors of Hercules: Part One

After killing his family in an insane rage induced by Hera [HEE-ruh], Hercules [HER-kue-leez] went to Eurystheus [yur-EES-thee-uhs], the king of Mycenae, and offered to be his slave. He was prepared to accept the most difficult tasks as punishment for his crime. Eurystheus invented twelve tasks, known as the Twelve Labors. They were all nearly impossible to accomplish, even for the strongest man on earth.

Hera = Juno
Hercules = Heracles

The First Labor was to kill the Nemean Lion. In the Nemean Valley near Mycenae, a terrible lion ranged. Hercules went there, taking his bow and quiver of arrows and the big club he always had with him. He found the lion's den, but the beast was out hunting, so Hercules waited. At the end of the day the lion came back licking its slavering chops, spotted with the blood of its prey. Hercules shot an arrow, but it bounced off the beast's hide, for this was a special lion—it could not be killed with conventional weapons. Only Hercules' incredible strength could conquer the beast. He slammed his club over the lion's head; the club splintered but momentarily stunned the beast. Hercules jumped on its back, worked down the hind legs with his feet, grabbed the lion's neck with his hands, drew back the head, and strangled him. He cut off the tawny hide with the lion's own claws and took it back with him, but would not give it up to Eurystheus. He had won it as a trophy of war in a fair fight, which none could deny, and he wore it afterwards with the head on his own head like a helmet.

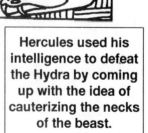

The Second Labor concerned the Lernaean Hydra. This was a beast, a big snake, with nine heads. The Hydra lived way off in the swamps and marshes of Argos, near the sea. Hercules rode to the place in his chariot, driven by his nephew Iolaus [i-oh-LAY-uhs]. When they got there, the hero tried several weapons: arrows, his club, and a sickle. He cut off one head after another, but whenever he had severed one, two more grew in its place.

A huge crab came to help the Hydra, and young Iolaus ran up to help

Hercules used his intelligence to defeat the Hydra by coming up with the idea of cauterizing the necks of the beast.

© Mark Twain Media, Inc., Publishers

his uncle. But the heroes, though holding their own, were not getting anywhere until Hercules suddenly became inspired. He told his nephew to build a fire and set up torches. As his uncle lopped off a Hydra head, Iolaus cauterized the neck with fire to close it so that no new head could grow. After cutting off the last head and searing the neck with fire, they buried the head under a rock. The marsh still breeds snakes, but they are just ordinary ones, mean but not monsters. The heroes killed the Hydra's crab ally, too, and it became a constellation in the sky, part of the zodiac group that terrified Phaethon [FAY-eh-thon].

The Third Labor was to capture the Arcadian Deer. This deer was female, a doe, but it bore antlers of gold and had feet of bronze. Being sacred to Artemis [AR-tem-is], she wandered free all over wooded Arcady,

Artemis = Diana

and it took Hercules a year of hunting before he caught her. On the return trip, with the live deer strapped to his back, he ran into Artemis, who angrily asked what he was doing with *her* doe. Hercules answered meekly that he had no choice; it was the will of Zeus expressed through the oracle that as a penance he obey Lord Eurystheus in all things. So he made his peace with Artemis, who was not easily appeased.

In the Fourth Labor, Hercules took on the Erymanthian Boar. This beast was a menace to the whole country: people, livestock, and crops. Hercules' task was to capture the boar and take it to King Eurystheus.

On his way to find the boar, Hercules had to pass through the land of the Centaurs, those rather engaging creatures with a man's head and shoulders and a horse's body. They had the strength and speed of horses and the wisdom of men, but most of them were more beasts than men. There was one, however, Pholus [FOH-luhs] by name, who was friendly. When Hercules arrived, Pholus invited him into his cave for a drink of punch and a good meal. The hero thanked the Centaur for his hospitality and went in. Pholus served him the punch; it was delicious. Hercules had never tasted anything like it before. The aroma spread near and far, and the other Centaurs came galloping up. When they discovered Hercules enjoying their special punch, they attacked him. Pholus, scared nearly to death, ran off, so Hercules had to take on these wild beasts alone. They went at him

Artemis was angry with Hercules for capturing the Arcadian Deer.

© Mark Twain Media, Inc., Publishers   66

with torn up trees, big boulders, torches, and axes. Their mother, a big storm cloud, poured down a gray fog like pea soup that blinded Hercules and made the cave floor so slippery he could hardly stand up. But he persisted in the fight, wiping out a good many of the Centaurs and driving the rest away.

Hercules continued his search for the wild boar. When he found the boar he chased it all around the bushes in the snow until the brute died of pure exhaustion. Hercules threw it across his back like a large rucksack and tramped into the hall where king Eurystheus was waiting, always ready with more work for him to do.

Beyond the Myth

1. How did Hercules use different weapons and tactics for each Labor?

2. Imagine what it would be like to be a Centaur. What would be the advantages and disadvantages of being half human and half horse?

Identify:

Iolaus	Hydra
Pholus	Centaur

Define:

cauterize   slavering   tawny

Locate on a map:

Mycenae	Nemean Valley	Argos
Arcadia (Arcady)	Erymanthia	

Name _____ Date _____

The Twelve Labors of Hercules: Part One

1. As punishment for killing his family, Hercules went to _____, the King

of Mycenae, and offered to be his slave.

2. The First Labor was the killing of the Nemean _____.

3. How did Hercules conquer this beast? _____

_____

_____

4. The Second Labor concerned the Lernaean _____ , a snake with nine

_____ .

5. With his nephew, _____ , Hercules took on this beast. When the heads kept

coming back, he got the bright idea of_____, or sealing, the stumps of the

necks with fire.

6. The heroes also killed the Hydra's ally, a huge _____.

7. The Third Labor was the pursuit of the Arcadian _____.

8. This animal was sacred to _____ .

9. In the Fourth Labor, Hercules took on the Erymanthian _____. While searching for

it he had an encounter with the_____.

10. Hercules killed the Erymanthian beast by _____

_____

_____ .

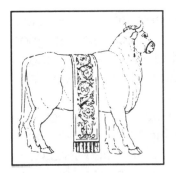

The Twelve Labors of Hercules: Part Two

The Fifth Labor, the chore of cleaning out the Augean stables, was less dangerous than some of the others, but in its way even more arduous. Augeas [oh-JEE-uhs] was king of neighboring Elis. His stable, with thousands of cattle, had not been cleaned for thirty years, so it was incredibly filthy. Hercules [HER-kue-leez] was told to clean it all up in a single day. Hercules for once was shrewd. He said he'd do the job, but Augeas would have to give him one-tenth of the cattle. Augeas agreed.

Hercules = Heracles

Now Hercules proved himself to be a clever engineer, a master of hydraulics. There were two rivers nearby, one on each side of the stable. Hercules knocked out parts of the stable walls at either end and diverted the course of both rivers toward the upper end of the barn. Following the natural line of gravity, the rivers ran downhill, converged, and ripped through the stalls, washing away all of the dirt and filth.

Augeas, however, went back on his promise of the cows. Hercules did not argue; he was still consumed with working out his penance. But later he took his revenge by seizing riches from Elis, which he used to found the ancient Olympic games.

Hercules watches as the rivers clean the Augean stables for him.

The Sixth Labor was to eliminate the Stymphalian birds. These were man-eating birds with claws, beaks, and wings of bronze. They came out of Lake Stymphalus in Arcadia, swarmed down on the fields, and destroyed

Athena = Minerva

Athena

crops like locusts. For this task, Hercules received help from the goddess Athena [uh-THEEN-uh], who respected him for his manliness and good heart. She gave him a big brass rattle that sounded like a whole band of cymbals. Assaulted by the tremendous noise, the bronze birds flew off, and Hercules shot them with his poisoned arrows.

The Seventh Labor was to deliver the Cretan bull to King Eurystheus [yur-EES-thee-uhs]. The Cretan bull belonged to King Minos [MY-nohs] of Crete. It was a beautiful creature, but it had gone crazy, and King Minos was anxious to get rid of it. Hercules went to Crete, captured the mad bull, and took it back to Mycenae.

The next Labor, the Eighth, was to capture the wild mares of Diomedes [die-oh-MEE-deez], a barbarian king of Thrace. His horses were man eaters and so wild that Diomedes had to tether them to their brass mangers with chains of iron. Hercules organized a troop of young men and led them to Thrace, where they made a massive assault on Diomedes' citadel, which soon fell. They captured the cruel and savage king, and the horses, no longer threatened by this evil man, calmed down and were easily led to Eurystheus.

Beyond the Myth

1. What is the broader sense behind the phrase, "Cleaning the Augean stables"? In 1992, presidential candidate Ross Perot stated it was time to "clean out the barn." What did he mean by that?

Identify:

Augean stables	Stymphalian birds
The Cretan Bull	Wild Mares of Diomedes

Define:

hydraulics   converge   citadel

Locate on a map:

Elis   Arcadia   Crete   Mycenae   Thrace

© Mark Twain Media, Inc., Publishers

Name_____ Date _____

The Twelve Labors of Hercules: Part Two

1. The Fifth Labor involved cleaning the _____ _____ .

2. To do this Hercules caused two _____ to run downhill.

3. Augeas went back on his promise to give Hercules _____ of the cows.

4. Later, Hercules took his revenge on Augeas by seizing riches from Elis. With this he started the

famous_____ _____ .

5. The Sixth Labor was a battle with the Stymphalian _____ .

6. This time Hercules didn't really have to fight; he just scared them off with a big _____.

7. The Seventh Labor was to deliver the bull from _____ to King Eurystheus.

8. The bull's owner, King _____ of Crete, was anxious to be rid of it.

9. The Eighth Labor was to capture the _____ _____ of

_____ .

10. How did Hercules get the horses to calm down? _____

_____

© Mark Twain Media, Inc., Publishers

The Twelve Labors of Hercules: Part Three

Hercules = Heracles

Labor Number Nine involved the beautiful belt of Hippolyta [hip-PAW-lit-uh], Queen of the Amazons, a tribe of women warriors who fought on horseback. Hercules [HER-kue-leez] raised another army of volunteers and led it across the Aegean Sea into Asia Minor. At first he tried tough diplomacy and simply demanded the belt. Surprisingly, Hippolyta seemed willing to give it up; she may have been impressed by this brisk and brusque young soldier. The other Amazons, however, thought their queen was being taken captive, so they attacked the Greeks. It was quite a battle: Europe against Asia, men against women! But Hercules' men won, and Hercules brought the broad belt back.

The Tenth Labor involved the longest journey, to an island, Erythia, located off the Spanish Coast, where there lived a dreadful monster, Geryon [GAIR-ee-on], who had three bodies joined at the waist. Another, lesser, monster guarded his cattle, along with a two-headed dog. These beasts were laying waste to all the lands in the area, creating a state of disorder without any effective government. Hercules' job was to bring back Geryon's cattle.

On his way to battle the monster, Hercules built two gigantic pillars, one on either side of the straits that are now called Gibraltar, where the Mediterranean Sea meets the Atlantic Ocean. For thousands of years these pillars were called the Pillars of Hercules.

When he arrived on the island, he killed the two-headed dog with his club, then killed the guardian monster and shot the three-bodied Geryon with arrows. He drove the cattle back by a land route through Europe. He also taught the people of the island the ways of law and stable government—a great accomplishment for a man who had been

Amazons were fierce women warriors who lived in Asia Minor.

a slow learner in school!

The Eleventh Labor was to fetch the Golden Apples of the Hesperides, guarded by the three fair daughters of Atlas [AT-luhs] along with a great dragon. This task was even more difficult because he did not know exactly

where the Hesperides were, so he had to hunt all over the known world and even into the unknown world. At first, he went the wrong way, to the east, as far as the Caucasus Mountains, where Prometheus [pro-MEE-thee-uhs], the great Titan who gave fire to mankind, was still bound to the icy rock, still suffering terrible torments. Here the anger of Hercules at the Titan's unjust fate was a righteous anger, and here perhaps he did his greatest deed, though it is not officially ranked with the Twelve. He set Prometheus free. Only the strongest man in the world—not even a god—could have done that. Hercules even proved to be a successful diplomat—he persuaded Zeus to take Prometheus back again and treat him kindly and receive him well at Olympus.

> **While Atlas went to find the Golden Apples of the Hesperides, Hercules held up the sky.**

Prometheus wished to return the favor as best he could. He counseled Hercules to find Atlas, his brother, and ask him where the apples were, since the Hesperides were his daughters. Hercules did so. He found the old Titan on his mountain in northwest Africa, holding up the sky. Hercules, in a friendly way, greeted him and asked directions. Atlas said, regretfully, that the exact location of the garden was a secret. "But," he said, "just hold up the sky for me, and I'll get the apples for you." Hercules agreed and took the skies on his shoulders, while Atlas, delighted to be free, ran off to fetch the apples. Holding up the heavens was a tough chore even for Hercules, and he began to wonder if perhaps he had made a mistake. But Atlas was true to his word; he brought the apples back. A little wistfully, he asked if he might deliver them to Eurystheus [yur-EES-thee-uhs]. But

© Mark Twain Media, Inc., Publishers

Hercules was afraid that if Atlas went off with the apples he would never come back, and then Hercules would have to hold up the skies until the end of time. So he asked the giant to hold up the sky for just a minute while he eased his shoulders. "After all," he told him, "even strong men need to rest." Atlas was not smart like his brother, Prometheus—he had no foresight. So he agreed. Hercules put the sky back on the Titan's shoulders, picked up the apples, and took them back to Eurystheus.

Pluto = Hades

For his Twelfth Labor, Hercules was required to go down to Hades and fetch up Cerberus [SER-ber-uhs], the three-headed dog who guarded the door. Pluto [PLOO-toh] was willing to loan out his dog for awhile, but forbade Hercules to use weapons. So the hero grabbed the dog in his hands and gave him several good squeezes until he was tamed. Then he carried him to the upper world, showed him to Eurystheus, and brought him back. With that, Hercules' labors were done.

Beyond the Myth

1. How do the later Labors show that Hercules is growing in maturity, perception, and judgment?

2. Compare Hercules' encounters with Prometheus and Atlas.

Identify:

Hippolyta	Pillars of Hercules
Geryon	Apples of the Hesperides
Atlas	Cerberus

Define: brusque   foresight

Locate on a map:

Aegean Sea	Spain	Asia Minor (Turkey)
Mediterranean Sea	Atlantic Ocean	Pillars of Hercules (Gibraltar)
Caucasus Mountains	Africa	Atlas Mountains

© Mark Twain Media, Inc., Publishers

Name_____ Date _____

The Twelve Labors of Hercules: Part Three

1. The Ninth Labor was to bring back the beautiful _____ of Hippolyta, Queen of

the _____ .

2. The other Amazons thought Hippolyta was being taken _____ , so they attacked

the Greeks.

3. This involved a battle between _____ and _____ .

4. The Tenth Labor was to bring back the _____ of the monster Geryon.

5. On his way to battle Geryon, the three-bodied monster, Hercules built two gigantic pillars.

For a long time these were called the _____ of _____ ; today

the area is called the Straits of _____ .

6. The Eleventh Labor was to fetch the _____ _____ of

the Hesperides.

7. In his search, Hercules found _____ and released him from his

rock.

8. He even persuaded _____ to receive Prometheus at Olympus.

9. Hercules got _____ to fetch the _____ for him while he held

up the _____ .

10. The Twelfth Labor, and the last, was a journey to Hades to bring up Cerberus, the three-

headed _____ .

Name _____ Date _____

HERCULES CROSSWORD

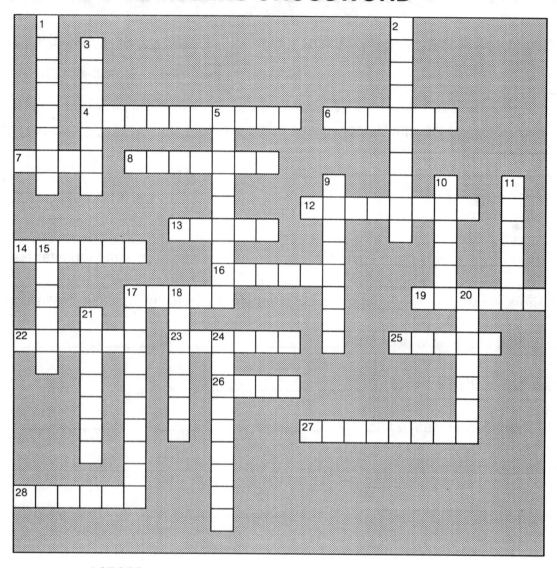

ACROSS

4. King of Mycenae
6. Lion killed by Hercules
7. Hercules' goddess enemy
8. Games started by Hercules
12. Our hero
13. He held up the sky
14. She convinced Hercules to work hard in life
16. Number of Hercules' labors
17. Big snake with nine heads
19. Baby Hercules killed these in his bed
22. He had a filthy stable
23. Hercules' wife
25. King Minos's bull lived here
26. Hercules chased it through the snow until it died
27. Greek name for Hercules
28. A friendly centaur

DOWN

1. Wicked owner of the wild mares
2. Hercules set him free
3. Eurystheus was king there
5. Queen of the Amazons
9. Three-headed guard dog
10. He had three bodies joined at the waist
11. Hercules used it to get rid of the Stymphalian birds
15. Hercules' nephew
17. They owned the Golden Apples
18. Child of a god and a mortal
20. She was very fond of the Arcadian deer
21. Part man, part horse
24. The Pillars of Hercules are now called the Straits of _____

© Mark Twain Media, Inc., Publishers

Perseus and Medusa

King Acrisius [uh-KRIS-ee-uhs] of Argos had one child, his daughter Danaë [dan-AY-ee], who was good and beautiful. But Acrisius wanted a son, so he made a journey to the Delphic oracle to ask if he would ever be the father of a boy. The priestess said no, but his daughter Danaë would have a son, and that son would kill him. To prevent this, Acrisius shut Danaë up in a bronze underground apartment with an open roof to let in light and air. The poor prisoner was cut off from men, but Zeus [ZOOS], drawn by her beauty, came to her through the open roof in the form of a shower of gold and made her his bride. Then he left her. Time passed, and one day a messenger came running to Acrisius and panted out, "Majesty, a son is borne to your daughter!" The king, aghast and scared, had a big chest made. Danaë and the baby boy, Perseus [PER-see-uhs], were placed in the chest and set adrift on the sea.

Zeus = Jupiter, Jove

By wind and wave they drifted to the tiny island of Seriphus. A fisherman, Dictys [DIK-tis], who was tending his nets, found the chest on the beach and released the prisoners. Dictys was a good man. He took the woman and the baby home to his wife. As they had no children of their own, they were delighted to have Danaë and Perseus stay with them. Perseus grew up tall, strong, and athletic—in all ways a princely young man.

Zeus, king of the gods, was Perseus's father.

Dictys had a brother, Polydectes [paw-lee-DEK-teez], King of Seriphus, who was a cruel and wicked man. The lovely Danaë and her handsome son drew his attention. He offered to marry the lady, but she, already the bride of Zeus, refused. Polydectes bullied her, but he feared Perseus. He developed a plan that he was sure would lead to the young man's death. He flattered the lad for his prowess at the games, his skill at boxing and with the discus. He told Perseus he was wasting his talents on Seriphus. There was a big world out there; he should go see it and do great deeds and become a hero.

"How could I become a hero?" asked Perseus.

Polydectes replied, coolly, "Go kill the Gorgon, Medusa [meh-DOO-suh] of the snaky locks, and bring me her head."

© Mark Twain Media, Inc., Publishers

77

The king explained to Perseus that there were three sisters, called Gorgons, living somewhere far away in the west in the land of darkness. Two were very ugly, but Medusa was most beautiful. However, her hair of coiling serpents was so terrible the sight of it turned men to stone. No one knew exactly where these horrible sisters lived.

Athena = Minerva

Hades = Pluto

Hermes = Mercury

The hero needed all the help of the gods, and he got it. Athena [uh-THEEN-uh] gave him her strong shield, so highly polished it was like a mirror. Hades [HAY-deez] gave his helmet that made the wearer invisible. Hermes [HER-meez] brought a pair of silver sandals with bright wings. They also gave him a special weapon, a sword with a curved blade, like a sickle. But there were no guidelines for him to get there. Athena told him he must find the Gray Sisters, who would tell him where to go.

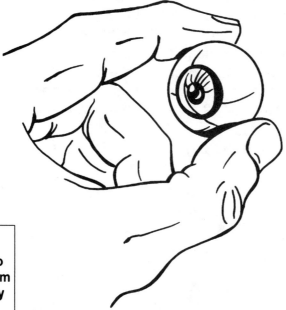

Hermes was his guide for the first stretch of the journey . They flew over the seas to the black-earth country of the Cimmerians (now called the Ukraine, located in southern Russia). In that wild twilight zone of the northern borderlands they found the Gray Sisters. They were like three old gray birds,who had only one eye and one tooth between them, which they passed around. Perseus had to trick them into telling him what he wanted to know by stealing the eye; then he

The Gray Sisters shared one eye, so Perseus tricked them into helping him by stealing their eye.

returned it to them with thanks. He and Hermes flew on, east of the sun and west of the moon, to the very limits of the earth: the back of the North Wind. This was the blessed land of the Hyperboreans, who lived happy in a climate of never-ending spring, feasting and dancing to the tunes of lyre and pipes. They gave Perseus a big leather wallet, which would always stretch to the right size for anything in it. So, with Athena's shield, Pluto's invisible helmet, Hermes' sandals, and his sickle sword, Perseus was ready for Medusa.

Alone now, he flew off to the far west and found the Gorgons' cave as the Gray Sisters had told him. Outside near the entrance were statues of men, their stone faces set in expressions of terror. With his back to the cave, Perseus kept his eyes on Athena's shield which, shining like a mirror, reflected the shapes of the Gorgons who were sleeping inside. Two of them were ugly things, though decorated in gold and bronze, with curved, cruel claws and huge teeth. They were immortals, and Perseus could have done nothing to them. But the third sister, Medusa, was mortal and beautiful, though a bit pale, and it would have been hard to find her in the darkness—

Hermes

© Mark Twain Media, Inc., Publishers   78

except for the whispering sounds of the serpents that were her hair. Silently thanking the gods for the invisible helmet, Perseus backed into the cave, watching the images in the mirrored surface of his shield. Focusing on the reflection of Medusa's head, he rose a bit on the winged sandals, raised the sword above him, and Athena, who was always there at the right time, guided his hand. With one sweeping blow, the curved blade cut off the snaky head, and Perseus dropped it into the leather bag, drawing the latches tight—but not before he had spilled some blood. From those drops sprang the winged horse, Pegasus [PEG-uh-suhs]. But Perseus was already in the air. The other two sisters woke up and ran raving and screaming after him, their golden wings clattering, bronze claws slashing. But Perseus, victorious, was gone.

> **With the help of the gods, Perseus was able to kill the Gorgon, Medusa.**

Beyond the Myth

Compare the journeyings of Perseus with those of one of the other heroes.

Identify:

Perseus	Medusa	The "shower of gold"
Danaë	The Gray Sisters	Hyperboreans
Gorgons	Dictys	Polydectes

Define:

sickle	oracle	prowess

Locate on a map:

Argos	Seriphus Island	Ukraine

© Mark Twain Media, Inc., Publishers

79

Name _____   Date _____

Perseus and Medusa

1. Acrisius of Argos had a daughter, _____.

2. Zeus came to her in a shower of _____.

3. Acrisius had mother and child put in a _____ and set adrift. They floated

to the little island of Seriphus.

4. They were rescued by a good fisherman, _____. His brother, Polydectes, was

the wicked _____ of the island.

5. To find and kill the Gorgon, Perseus needed all the help he could get. Athena gave him her

_____, Pluto his _____ , and Hermes his winged_____.

6. With Hermes as guide, the hero flew to the black-earth country of the Cimmerians,

present-day _____ (southern Russia). Here they found the _____

_____.

7. Next they flew to the happy land of the Hyperboreans, who never suffered from cold because

they lived at the back of the _____ _____.

8. Outside the Gorgon's cave, to avoid looking directly at Medusa, Perseus used his

_____ as a mirror.

9. He was lucky to be wearing an _____ helmet.

10. From the blood of Medusa sprang the winged horse, _____.

© Mark Twain Media, Inc., Publishers

Perseus and Andromeda

Perseus [PER-see-uhs], having severed the snaky-haired head of Medusa [meh-DOO-suh] from her body, began his journey home. He came first to the mountains of northwest Africa where he found the old Titan, Atlas [AT-luhs], holding up the heavens and growing weary with that never-ending chore. Atlas greeted Perseus with pleasure; he had already learned from an oracle what the hero had been up to and that Perseus was fated to relieve his burden and set him free. "You know," he said, "I've never had any time off, except when Hercules paid me a visit and relieved me to go fetch the golden apples of the Hesperides." He sighed. "I'm tired of this job, it's too much even for a Titan. Please show me the Gorgon's head." Perseus understood and sympathized. With his own head turned away, he drew the dreadful head of Medusa out of the leather bag and showed it to Atlas, then returned it to the bag. He watched as the Titan changed. Atlas, already large, grew larger; his hips thrust out into the foothills of mighty mountains, and his shoulders became their lofty summits. His beard and hair turned into thick forests. His head, turning to stone, reared up among the clouds and stars; his gigantic hands and arms steadied the skies. The Titan had become part of the range that is still called the Atlas Mountains.

Perseus was fated to have one more grand adventure. As he flew east he came to a stretch of African seacoast that lies along Abyssinia (Ethiopia). Here he found a lovely maiden in a white tunic, chained to a rock. Perseus flew down close. "Maiden," he said, hovering, "who does not deserve these chains, who are you? What is your country? Why are you being punished in this cruel way?"

> **Andromeda was being punished for her mother's foolish boasting.**

"Sir," the beauty replied, "I am Andromeda [an-DROM-eh-duh], Princess of Abyssinia." She explained that she was being sacrificed to a terrible sea dragon because the gods were angry with her mother, Cassiopeia [kas-ee-oh-PEE-uh]. This foolish queen had boasted that she was more beautiful than the daughters of Poseidon [poh-SIE-don], the Sea God. The Nereids, of course, were furious, but their wrath fell not on the vain mother but on the innocent daughter. The sea dragon was devouring youths and

Poseidon = Neptune

© Mark Twain Media, Inc., Publishers

81

maidens all along the coast. If Andromeda were given to him, he would depart, satisfied.

Even as the princess talked, they heard a roaring sound and saw the monster, green and scaly, rapidly gliding toward them across the sea. Perseus leaped into the air, and as the dragon drew near he came down hard and from behind, gashing the beast's neck and shoulder. An awful fight followed; Andromeda shut her eyes in terror. The dragon split huge

rocks with his lashing tail, which cracked like a whip. Perseus came at him again and again, working under the scales with his sickle blade, until the dreadful thing at last lay lifeless on the rocks and sand, its tail floating out to sea. The hero loosened the maiden's chains and took her back to her father, King Cepheus [SEE-fee-uhs], who was quite willing to give Andromeda to Perseus as his wife.

It was a beautiful and happy wedding, but before Perseus could settle down to married life, he had to hurry back to Seriphus and hand Medusa's head to Polydectes [paul-ee-DEK-teez]. When he got to Seriphus, he found his mother, Danaë [dan-AY-ee], and his good foster father, Dictys [DIK-tis], taking refuge in a temple. King Polydectes had been harassing them. While Danaë was explaining what had happened, the king appeared at the head of a band of soldiers. When he saw Perseus had come back, his false smile grew sickly. "Did you get the Gorgon?" he demanded. For answer, Perseus loosened the leather bag and flashed Medusa's head at the wicked king; he and his soldiers became frozen statues.

Perseus killed the sea dragon that was sent to devour Andromeda.

Hades = Pluto
Athena = Minerva
Hermes = Mercury

Perseus gave back the helmet to Hades [HAY-deez], the shield to Athena [uh-THEEN-uh], and the winged sandals to Hermes [HER-meez], with profound thanks to all the gods. He made the good Dictys king of the island of Seriphus. He sent for his bride, Andromeda, and decided to take her, with Danaë, back to Greece to see if they could reconcile with his grandfather, King Acrisius [uh-KRIS-ee-uhs] of Argos, who had sent him and his mother adrift in a sea chest when he was an infant.

They found the king in the North where his host, the King of Larissa, was throwing a series of parties and athletic games. Perseus was a good-hearted youth and quite prepared to forgive his grandfather and treat him kindly. But the oracle had spoken. One day Perseus decided to participate

© Mark Twain Media, Inc., Publishers

in the discus-throwing; Acrisius was standing by as a spectator. The hero took up the heavy bronze plate and pitched it far, but it was a curved throw and flew off to the side where it struck Acrisius in the head and killed him.

As for the terrible Gorgon's head, Perseus gave it to Athena, who had helped him so much. An effigy, or image, of it was carved into the aegis, Zeus's [ZOOS-ez] shield, which Athena carried for him.

Zeus = Jupiter, Jove

Andromeda in time became a constellation, as did Perseus, Cepheus, and Cassiopeia—the whole family raised to the stars!

Athena

Zeus

Identify:

| Atlas Mountains | Cassiopeia |
| Nereids | Andromeda |

Define:

effigy   aegis   discus

Locate on a map:

Atlas Mountains   Larissa

© Mark Twain Media, Inc., Publishers

Name _____ Date _____

Perseus and Andromeda

1. In North Africa Perseus found the old Titan, _____, still holding up the sky and getting

tired of it. Perseus helped him out by showing him the head of Medusa and turning him to

_____ .

2. Traveling east, he came to a stretch of seacoast along the country of _____ .

Here he found the maiden, _____ , daughter of King _____

and Queen _____ .

3. The queen had offended the _____ , daughters of the sea god.

4. Perseus killed the sea dragon by working under its _____ with his curved blade.

5. After marrying the princess, Perseus returned to Seriphus to hand _____ 's head

to Polydectes.

6. Perseus punished King Polydectes by turning him and his soldiers to _____ .

7. Perseus still wanted to reconcile with King Acrisius of _____ .

8. But the prophecy of the Delphic oracle had to be fulfilled. Without intending to, Perseus killed

his evil grandfather with a heavy bronze_____ at an athletic contest in Larissa.

9. Perseus gave the Gorgon's head to _____ . An image of it was carved into

Zeus's shield, which is called the _____ .

10. Andromeda, Cassiopeia, Cepheus, and Perseus eventually became_____

in the heavens.

Bellerophon and Pegasus

When Perseus [PER-see-uhs] cut off the head of Medusa [meh-DOO-suh], a horse with wings sprang up from some drops of her blood. Named Pegasus [PEG-uh-suhs], he was a noble, marvelous horse of a shining bay color (reddish brown). His two wings were big enough to hide his rider and keep him warm from the wind—but he had never had a rider.

The man who would bridle, mount, and ride Pegasus was Bellerophon [bell-AIR-uh-fon]. He was a young prince of Corinth, handsome and brave. Bellerophon knew all about Pegasus, the wonder horse, whose stamping hoofs on the Muses' mountain of Helicon had caused Hippocrene, the sacred spring of poets, to bubble up from the ground. The young prince of Corinth yearned for that horse as he had never desired anything in his life.

The oracle of Corinth, old man Polyidus [paw-lee-I-duhs], counseled a visit to Athena's [uh-THEEN-uhz] temple, explaining that only the divine aid of the gods could capture a divine horse. Bellerophon prayed and slept in the temple; the goddess appeared and gave him a bit and bridle of gold. The next day he found the horse in the high pastures. He slipped the bridle over his head and the golden bit into his mouth. Pegasus was calm and did not resist. Then Bellerophon, wearing his bronze armor, leaped onto his back (there were no saddles or stirrups in those days). Never was a horse more quickly tamed.

Then trouble came. Bellerophon accidentally killed a man and needed to be purified by a king's touch. He went to King Proetus [pro-EE-tuhs] of Tiryns, made his confession and atonement, and was absolved.

But Anteia [an-TAY-uh], the wife of Proetus, fell in love with Bellerophon. He rejected her advances, but she told lies to her husband, saying that Bellerophon had dishonored her. King Proetus was in a bind: Bellerophon was a guest, and the king could not violate the laws of hospitality by killing him. So he sent him off with a letter to his brother-in-law Iobates [i-AHB-uh-teez], the king of Lycia. The letter was a request that Iobates kill Bellerophon at the first chance. But King Iobates was also reluctant to kill Bellerophon. Even more than Proetus, he was incapable of violating the laws that bind host and guest—Zeus [ZOOS] would be furious.

So Iobates sent Bellerophon off to fight the Chimaera [kie-MEE-ruh],

Athena

Athena = Minerva

With Athena's help, Bellerophon was able to tame and ride Pegasus.

Zeus = Jupiter, Jove

© Mark Twain Media, Inc., Publishers

Zeus

who had been laying waste to the land. This was a truly formidable monster, with a lion's head, the body of a goat, and the tail of a snake. Bellerophon took his best weapons—bow and arrows and spear. But his best weapon of all was actually the flying bay horse.

It was a tremendous encounter—the man and horse plunging down to attack the foul beast as it reared up, growling, bleating, and hissing from the filthy rocks of its den, each downward swoop a flurry of arrows or lunges and thrusts with the spear. The green smoke of the monster's breath almost blew them down. But Pegasus swept down once more, and Bellerophon launched one more thrust; he drove the spearhead down deep into the green blood of the beast. A few more thrusts and it lay dead, the corpse smoldering away in greenish dust and gray ashes.

The devastated land rejoiced, and Bellerophon joined the ranks of the real heroes. But after a time, hubris—excessive pride—proved too strong. Bellerophon thought he would ride Pegasus up to Mount Olympus and become immortal. However, immortality is only granted to those the gods choose. Pegasus, wise horse, knew this. He balked at the bridle and threw his rider, crippling him. Poor, lame Bellerophon wandered the earth he yearned to leave for the rest of his life, waiting for his winged horse to come back. But Pegasus was given a refuge in the Olympian stables with the fierce steeds of Zeus. He was honored to fetch Zeus his bolts of thunder and lightning.

Beyond the Myth

1. Have you read any other stories about horses that you especially like?

2. Write a myth of your own about the winged horse, Pegasus. It may be set in ancient or modern times. You may include any of the other mythical characters or creatures you have learned about, or make up your own.

Identify:

Medusa	Hippocrene	Proetus
Iobates	Anteia	Chimaera

Define:

bay (color)	formidable	bit	balked	bridle

Locate on a map:

Corinth	Mount Helicon	Tiryns

© Mark Twain Media, Inc., Publishers

Name _____   Date _____

Bellerophon and Pegasus

1. From the blood of the Gorgon, Medusa, sprang the winged horse,_____.

2. Bellerophon prayed and slept in the temple of _____; she gave him a

_____ and _____ of gold.

3. Bellerophon went to King_____ of Tiryns to be purged. The king's wife,

_____ , fell in love with him.

4. The king could not kill Bellerophon because it would be a violation of the laws of

_____.

5. Bellerophon was asked to take a letter to King _____ of _____.

6. If the king had killed Bellerophon, _____ would have been furious.

7. The Chimaera had the head of a _____, body of a_____,

and tail of a _____.

8. The winged horse was Bellerophon's best _____.

9. Having killed the Chimaera, Bellerophon was a hero. But _____, excessive

pride, proved his downfall. He tried to ride Pegasus up to _____ _____

to become immortal.

10. Pegasus was wiser, and he threw his rider. He stayed on in the stables of Olympus and helped

Zeus by fetching his bolts of _____ and _____ .

© Mark Twain Media, Inc., Publishers   87

The Trojan War: Part One

An epic poem is a long narrative that relates the deeds of heroes. Many of the stories of the Trojan War were compiled in an epic poem called the *Iliad* by the author Homer. They are among the oldest stories in literature.

While these tales are clearly mythological, historians believe there really was a Trojan war and that it took place about 1200 B.C. near the coast of Turkey. It might have been a trade war between different groups of Greek-speaking people for control of waters leading into the Black Sea.

The Apple of Discord

The struggle began when Eris [AIR-is], goddess of discord and quarreling, was not invited to the wedding of the hero Peleus [PEE-lee-uhs] and the sea-nymph Thetis [THEE-tis]. Eris threw among the revelers a golden apple inscribed "for the fairest." It rolled right up to where three goddesses were sitting: Hera [HEE-ruh], Athena [uh-THEEN-uh], and Aphrodite [af-roh-DIE-tee]. Of course, each goddess claimed it. Zeus [ZOOS] refused to be the judge of this Olympian beauty contest. He knew no matter how he decided he would never hear the end of it from the others. He told the goddesses to have Hermes [HER-meez] escort them to a mountain near Troy where Paris [PAIR-uhs], a son of King Priam [PRY-uhm], was watching the sheep. The king had sent him away because he had been warned that someday this boy would bring grief and ruin on his country. Paris was supposed to be a good judge of feminine beauty. The goddesses agreed, and Zeus warned them to abide by Paris's choice, however it went. Hermes escorted them to the high pastures of Troy where the shepherd-prince watched his flocks.

Each goddess promised Paris something if he would favor her. Hera offered him kingly power, Athena promised wisdom and glory in war, but Aphrodite, the Love Goddess, offered him the most beautiful woman in the world for his wife. Paris cared nothing for power and glory and, least of all, wisdom. He was young and shallow-minded. He awarded the golden apple to Aphrodite.

Hera = Juno
Athena = Minerva
Aphrodite = Venus
Zeus = Jupiter, Jove

Hermes = Mercury

Aphrodite promised Paris the most beautiful woman in the world if he would give her the golden apple.

Helen of Sparta

The most beautiful woman in the

© Mark Twain Media, Inc., Publishers

world, Helen of Sparta, was the daughter of Zeus and Princess Leda [LEE-duh]. Of course, every prince in Greece wanted to marry her. Her mother's new husband, King Tyndareus [tin-DAR-ee-uhs] of Sparta, had to choose among the suitors. He was afraid that whoever he chose would have to fight for Helen against all the rest. To prevent this, he made them all take an oath that they would accept his decision and support the cause of Helen's husband if any wrong were committed against him because of this marriage. The suitors, each thinking he might be the one chosen, swore the oath and promised solemnly to punish any man who interferred with the marriage. Tyndareus then chose Menelaus [men-eh-LAY-uhs], brother of Agamemnon [ag-uh-MEM-non], King of Mycenae, and made Menelaus a king of Sparta, too.

Helen of Sparta

Meanwhile, Aphrodite led Paris directly to Sparta. Menelaus and Helen received the Trojan prince graciously. They trusted him so completely that Menelaus went off on an expedition to Crete, leaving his wife to entertain their guest. The ties between host and guest among the Greeks were sacred, but Paris violated that trust, with the help of Aphrodite, who turned her arts on Helen and made her fall madly in love with the boy. When Menelaus got back he found his guest gone and his wife with him.

Here the oath and pact of the suitors went into effect. The brother of the injured husband, King Agamemnon of Mycenae, as commander in chief, was able to rally nearly all of the Greek kings to bring Helen back.

Beyond the Myth

If you had to choose, would you rather have power, money, honor, glory, wisdom and knowledge, or beauty? (Be honest!)

Identify:

Homer	Eris	Leda	Peleus
Paris	Thetis	Priam	Helen
Agamemnon	Menelaus		

Define: discord   revelers   suitors

Locate on a map:
Turkey   Troy   Mycenae   Black Sea   Sparta

© Mark Twain Media, Inc., Publishers

Name _____   Date _____

The Trojan War: Part One

1. Some of the oldest stories in literature are found in a poem called the *Iliad* by _____.

2. Historians believe there really was a Trojan war; it might have been a trade war for economic control of the waters leading into the _____ _____ .

3. Eris was the goddess of _____ and _____ .

4. The three rival goddesses for the beauty prize were _____ ,_____ , and _____ .

5. For a decision, Zeus sent them to the shepherd-prince, _____ , son of King _____ of Troy.

6. Hera offered him _____ , Athena offered _____ _____ , and Aphrodite offered _____ for his favor.

7. He gave the apple to _____ .

8. The most beautiful woman in the world was _____ of Sparta.

9. Out of all the suitors, King Tyndareus chose _____ to be Helen's husband.

10. When Paris came as a guest, Helen fell in love with him because of the tricks of the goddess _____.

11. The ties between _____ and _____ were sacred to the Greeks.

12. The commander in chief of the Greek armies was _____ , brother of Menelaus.

© Mark Twain Media, Inc., Publishers

The Trojan War: Part Two

Valiant Warriors

Agamemnon gathered together hundreds of ships and set sail for Troy. The ships carried many men brave in battle and some wise in counsel. Chief among them was Achilles [uh-KILL-eez], the greatest warrior and champion of all the Greeks.

The Greek kings and army were strong, but so were the defenders of Troy. King Priam [PRY-uhm] and Queen Hecuba [HEH-kue-buh] had many valiant sons ready both for attack and defense. But first and foremost there was Prince Hector [HEK-ter]. He was not only brave but noble—in every way a match for Achilles. In a sense, the whole outcome of the war hung on when, where, and how these two might meet. The Fates had revealed that each would die before Troy would be overthrown. Both heroes lived and fought under the shadow of certain death.

The gods, as they always do, took sides: Hera [HEE-ruh] and Athena [uh-THEEN-uh], who had lost out in the "beauty contest" were naturally for the Greeks. Poseidon [poh-SIE-don], Sea God, also favored the Greeks. Aphrodite [af-roh-DIE-tee], Artemis [AR-tem-is], and Ares [AIR-eez] were for the Trojans. Zeus [ZOOS] and Apollo [uh-PAW-loh], who as a healer and physician did not favor war, were neutral.

And so the Trojan War would shake both heaven and earth.

It went on for nine years, the fighting swaying back and forth—a stalemate. The Greeks could not take Troy, and the Trojans could not drive out the Greeks.

Greek Warrior

Hera = Juno
Athena = Minerva
Poseidon = Neptune
Aphrodite = Venus
Artemis = Diana
Ares = Mars
Zeus = Jupiter, Jove
Apollo = Apollo

The Death of Patroclus and the Rousing of Achilles

One evening Achilles waited by his tent for his friend Patroclus [PAT-roh-kluhs] to come back from the day's fighting. He had loaned Patroclus his armor. But when he saw Antilochus [an-tee-LO-kuhs] running toward him, tears running down his face, he knew something was terribly wrong.

"Bad news, oh, bad news!" cried Antilochus. "Patroclus is slain; Hector has his armor."

Wild grief seized Achilles. He was filled with rage and anger at the death of his dearest friend. So black and bitter was his

Heroes of the Trojan War: Odysseus, Hector, and Achilles

mood that those around him feared for his life. Down in the sea caves his mother, Thetis [THEE-tis], heard his lament and came up to comfort him. He told her that if he could not avenge his comrade he was no longer worthy to live among men. "Remember," she said, "you are fated to die after Hector." "I care not," he replied. "I did not help my friend when he needed me. I will slay his destroyer. Then I can accept my own death without remorse."

Hephaestus = Vulcan

Hephaestus

Hephaestus [hee-FES-tuhs], at the request of Thetis, forged a new suit of mail and new weapons for Achilles. The shield was a marvel. The blacksmith god made it a work of art, with pictures and engravings of the earth and high heavens, the sea, sun, and moon, and the signs of the Zodiac and major constellations: the Pleiades and Orion and the Big Bear (Callisto). Also engraved on the shield were two beautiful cities, showing all the life of a Greek city of that time, with marriage feasts and dancing and law courts. It was a marvelous shield, indeed. When Thetis presented it to her son, Achilles was filled with great joy.

Beyond the Myth

1. Explain how the Trojan war "would shake both heaven and earth."

2. Using the description provided above, draw a picture of what you think Achilles' new shield looks like.

Identify:

the Pleiades	Orion	the Big Bear
Priam	Hecuba	Hector
Patroclus	Achilles	Thetis
Hephaestus		

Define:

valiant   neutral   stalemate   suit of mail

Locate on a map:

Troy

© Mark Twain Media, Inc., Publishers

Name _____ Date _____

The Trojan War: Part Two

1. The greatest of the Greek warriors was _____ .

2. The bravest and most noble of the Trojan warriors was Prince _____, son of Priam

and Hecuba.

3. Patroclus borrowed Achilles' armor, which was stolen by _____ after he

killed Patroclus.

4. Achilles was told the terrible news of Patroclus's death by _____ .

5. His mother, _____ , the sea-nymph, came to comfort him.

6. When Achilles swore revenge, she reminded him that his own _____ would

follow soon after that of Hector.

7. His mother got _____ , the blacksmith god, to forge a new suit of armor.

8. The smith made him a beautiful shield with signs of the Zodiac and some of the important

constellations, including the _____ , _____ , and the _____

_____ (Callisto).

The Trojan War: Part Three

The Death of Hector and the Ransoming of His Body

Achilles [uh-KILL-eez], wearing his new armor, left his tent and went to where his comrades and special troops, the Myrmidons, were waiting. They gazed at him with admiration and awe. Their need for him was desperate. Many of the soldiers were either wounded or exhausted.

The Trojans, under Hector [HEK-ter], fought gallantly, desperately, and madly. Even the great river of Troy, called Xanthus or Scamander, took part and tried to drown Achilles as he crossed it. But it was all in vain—the Champion of the Greeks came on, killing all who stood in his way, looking for Hector. The gods were fighting too. Athena [uh-THEEN-uh], War Goddess, knocked down Ares [AIR-eez], War God. Hera [HEE-ruh] grabbed Artemis's [AR-tem-is-iz] bow away from the Huntress and boxed her ears with it, as she had wanted to do for some time. Poseidon [poh-SIE-don] jeered at Apollo [uh-PAW-loh] and dared him to strike first, but Apollo wisely refused. He knew what Fate had in store for Hector—why struggle?

Zeus [ZOOS] watched the fracas from above and chuckled to see god fighting god, civil war within his Olympian family. How he had tried to keep them in order!

By now the great Scaean gates of Troy were thrown open, and the people—soldiers and citizens—were streaming into the town. Only Hector, bound by Fate, took his stand before the walls. From the top of the gate, his old father, Priam [PRY-uhm], and mother, Hecuba [HEH-kue-buh], called down to him to save himself and come inside, but he wouldn't listen. He had a task to perform for the honor of his country, regardless of the danger to himself.

Athena = Minerva
Ares = Mars
Hera = Juno
Artemis = Diana
Poseidon = Neptune
Apollo = Apollo

Zeus = Jupiter, Jove

Achilles, wearing armor forged by a god, was able to defeat the Trojan Hector

Achilles threw his spear. Hector crouched and it flew over his head. Hector threw his spear and missed. Athena brought Achilles a fresh spear. Hector, drawing his sword, the only weapon he had, rushed his foe. It was no contest. Achilles wore armor, wrought by a god, which could not be pierced. Hector wore the armor he had taken from Patroclus that had once belonged to Achilles. The Greek champion knew of a small open spot in the neck of that armor. He drove his spearpoint into Hector's throat. Falling and dying, the Trojan hero begged that his body be returned to his parents. But Achilles steadfastly refused, and the valiant soul of Hector took flight for Hades.

Most of the gods, watching from above, were shocked and appalled by Achilles' refusal to return Hector's body to his family. Zeus was especially displeased. He sent Iris [I-ris], his rainbow-messenger, to poor, old Priam to tell this tragic king of Troy that he must ransom and redeem the body of his son. She was to tell the old man that Achilles was not really evil, but was overwrought by the death of his friend, Patroclus. If Priam went to him as humble petitioner, a *suppliant*, Achilles would receive him with courtesy and hear his plea.

Heeding the god's words, Priam filled a chariot with treasure and went to the Greek camp with Hermes [HER-meez] as his guide. Meanwhile, the funeral rites for Patroclus had been performed. These religious ceremonies had softened the heart of Achilles and cured him of his rage and grief. He now felt bad for not returning Hector's corpse, so he was in the right mood when Priam came into his presence, knelt down, embraced his knees, and kissed the hands that had killed his son.

Achilles' heart grew tender with grief. He received the old man with all kindness and respect. He guaranteed a truce for Hector's funeral rites and returned his body to Priam. He told his servants to anoint Hector's body with fragrant oil and cover it with a downy robe.

The mourning went on for nine days. Then they laid him on a high funeral pyre. When all was reduced to ashes, they put out the fire with wine and placed the bones in a golden funeral urn, then covered it in a purple shroud. They dug a grave and set the urn in it and covered it with big stones.

Hermes = Mercury

Hermes

Beyond the Myth

1. What does the fight between Achilles and Hector reveal about the characters of the two heroes? Who has the most advantage and why?

2. What has happened to Achilles between the death of Hector and Priam's visit to the Greek camp? Why do you suppose his mood changed?

3. Research funeral customs of other cultures. Are any of them similar to those described here?

Define:

suppliant	urn	ransom
funeral pyre	fracas	redeem

Locate on a map:
Xanthus (or Scamander) River

© Mark Twain Media, Inc., Publishers

Name _____ Date _____

The Trojan War: Part Three

1. The gods fight among themselves: Athena knocks down _____ , and

_____ beats _____ with her own bow.

2. The great _____ gate of Troy is thrown open, and the people pour into

town.

3. From the tower on top of the gate, _____ and _____ call out to their

son to save himself.

4. The armor that Hector wore had a small open spot in the _____ .

5. Achilles refused to return Hector's _____ to his parents.

6. Zeus sent his rainbow-messenger, _____ , to Priam telling him that to recover the

body of his son he must go to Achilles as a _____ .

7. By this time Achilles had been somewhat calmed and sobered by the _____ rites

of his friend Patroclus.

8. The mourning for Hector went on for_____ days.

9. The body was burned on a funeral _____ and the ashes placed in a golden

_____ .

10. They set the _____ in a grave and covered it with big _____ .

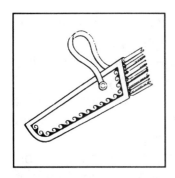

The Trojan War: Part Four

The Wooden Horse and the Fall of Troy

Even the longest wars must end sometime. The war between the Greeks and the Trojans ended finally after ten years—not by a decisive military victory, but by a strategic trick.

Hector [HEK-ter] was dead, and Achilles [uh-KILL-eez] knew his own end was near. He fought on and won more glory. But then, as the Greeks laid siege again to the city of Troy, Paris [PAIR-is], whose "judgment" had started the war, shot an arrow at him. Guided by Apollo [uh-PAW-loh], it flew true to the one spot where Achilles could be hurt—his heel. When he was a baby, his mother, Thetis [THEE-tis], had dipped him in the River Styx to make him invulnerable to weapons. She neglected, however, to dip the part of his foot by which she held him. So the Champion of the Greeks died of an infected, festering wound in the heel.

The only way to gain a victory would be to take the town of Troy by surprise. The great Greek warrior Odysseus [oh-DIS-see-uhs] developed the strategy of the wooden horse. He found a skilled artisan, a woodcarver, to make a wooden horse, hollow and big enough to hold a whole squad of men inside, including himself. The plan was for the other Greeks to dismantle the camp, take to the ships, and pretend to be sailing off for home. Instead, they would hide behind the nearest islands and headlands. A single Greek would be left behind with a story made up to persuade the Trojans to take the horse into the city without inspecting it too closely. In the darkest part of the night, the Greeks hidden in the horse would come out and open the city gates. Meanwhile, the main part of the army would come back and be ready by the wall.

When dawn came, the last day for Troy, the Trojans beheld two sights that amazed them: the deserted Greek camp and the enormous wooden horse by the Scaean gates. The horse rather frightened them, but the departure of the Greeks filled them with joy, and they began to feast and celebrate. The long, cruel war was over at last!

Then the Greek left behind, Sinon [SIE-non], appeared. They

Paris

Odysseus = Ulysses

Greek warriors hid inside the wooden horse until the Trojans let down their guard.

97

Athena = Minerva

Greek Warrior

Aphrodite = Venus

dragged him to King Priam [PRY-uhm] where, under questioning, he groaned and cried that he was a Greek no more. Athena [uh-THEEN-uh], he said, had been greatly angered by the theft of one of her statues by the Greek soldiers. An oracle had told the Greeks she could only be appeased with blood sacrifice. Poor Sinon had been chosen for the sacrifice, but at night he had escaped and hidden out in the marshes along the river until the ships sailed off. (Odysseus had invented this story.)

The Trojans, exhilarated by the end of the war, showed compassion to Sinon and brought him food and drink. Sinon went on to explain about the horse. It had been made as an offering to Athena, he told them. It had been made big so that the Trojans would find it hard to take it into the city. The Greeks hoped the Trojans would destroy it, bringing down the wrath of Athena upon them. But if somehow it could be taken into the city, it would win the favor of the goddess.

They dragged the horse to the gate and even knocked down part of the wall to give it more room. Once they had set it up inside they went on their way, feasting and rejoicing, feeling both exhilaration and exhaustion after ten years of war and siege.

At midnight, as the city slept, Odysseus and the other chiefs crept out of the horse and dropped down into the street. They threw the gates open wide; the Greek army waiting outside rushed in. They lit fires. They stationed small bands of warriors by each house. By the time the Trojans woke up and discovered the terrible truth, Troy was burning. In utter confusion, as they struggled out, putting on their armor, they were met by Greeks who cut them down.

By morning King Priam and all the Trojan princes and chieftains were dead except Aeneas [ee-NEE-uhs], saved by his mother, Aphrodite [af-roh-DIE-tee], the only god who helped a Trojan that day. Aeneas fought as long as he could, then he went to see to the safety of his own family: his father, his wife, and their little son. Guided by Aphrodite, the four of them

Trojans ran for their lives as the Greeks burned and looted the city.

© Mark Twain Media, Inc., Publishers

ran quickly through the flaming streets, Aeneas carrying his father on his back, clasping his son's hand, his wife hurrying along by their side. But in the fear and panic of that awful time, his wife was separated from the rest and lost. Aeneas got his father and son away through the gates and out into the open fields. Though he mourned the loss of his wife, he would live long and have many adventures, and his descendants would be the founders of a great city—Rome.

Aphrodite saved Helen, too. Menelaus [men-eh-LAY-ohs] had been looking for her through the streets of the burning city, his sword poised to kill her and avenge his honor. But when the Love Goddess brought her to him, his love for her overwhelmed him. Gladly he took her into his arms, and soon they would sail away together, back to Sparta.

So it happened that Troy—the fortress city that had withstood the attacks of the Greek heroes for ten years—was conquered by deceit and treachery.

Aphrodite Leading Aeneas to Safety

Beyond the Myth

In the last days of the Trojan War, are your sympathies more with the Greeks or with the Trojans? Explain.

Identify:

River Styx	The Wooden Horse
Sinon	Aeneas

Define:

Achilles' heel	invulnerable
artisan	pillage

© Mark Twain Media, Inc., Publishers

Name _____ Date _____

The Trojan War: Part Four

1. Achilles' mother, Thetis, had dipped him in the_____ _____ to make him

invulnerable to weapons.

2. A vulnerable spot somewhere is called an "Achilles' _____."

3. Achilles was killed by _____ .

4. Odysseus developed the idea of the _____ _____ .

5. The Greeks pretended to be _____

_____ .

6. One Greek, named _____ , was left behind.

7. He explained that the horse was an offering to _____ .

8. The Trojans brought the horse into the town. At midnight,_____ and other

Greeks hidden in the horse came out and opened the gates.

9. There followed pillage, burning, looting, and killing. Among the few who survived was

_____ , son of Aphrodite.

10. The King of Sparta, _____ , went looking for his former wife, _____,

to kill her for her desertion, but he decided to take her back when the goddess _____

brought her to him.

Name _____ Date _____

TROJAN WAR CROSSWORD

ACROSS

1. Hector stole Achilles', which Patroclus had borrowed
6. Helen was kidnapped from this city
9. The most beautiful woman
10. Only Trojan prince to survive the war
12. Priam's wife; Hector's mother
13. Achilles' friend who died by Hector's sword
14. He forged a splendid new shield for Achilles
16. Goddess of Love; she won the contest
22. Bravest Trojan warrior
26. River in which Achilles' mother dipped him
27. Achilles' special troops
28. A wooden one fooled the Trojans
29. Husband of Helen

DOWN

1. Menelaus's brother; king of Mycenae
2. He planned the wooden horse trick
3. Greek who was left behind
4. Achilles' vulnerable spot
5. Goddess of war; she lost the contest
7. Champion of the Greeks
8. It was "for the fairest"
11. Petitioner
15. Country where Trojan War may have actually occurred
17. He made the judgment that started the war
18. Some of the oldest stories in literature are found here
19. Uninvited wedding guest
20. Priam was king of this city
21. Author of the Trojan War stories
23. A long narrative poem
24. Zeus's wife; she lost the contest
25. King of Troy; Hector's father

© Mark Twain Media, Inc., Publishers

The Odyssey: Part One

Odysseus = Ulysses

Athena

Athena = Minerva

Poseidon = Neptune

In addition to the *Iliad*, Homer wrote another long poem about the adventures of the Greek hero Odysseus [oh-DIS-see-uhs], the King of Ithaca, as he journeyed home following the end of the Trojan War. This poem is called the *Odyssey*.

Ten years had gone by since the fall of Troy, and no one knew what had happened to Odysseus. His son, Telemachus [teh-LEM-uh-kuhs], had grown up, but did not have the authority to assert himself as king of Ithaca. He could not keep away the greedy suitors who wanted to marry his mother, Penelope [pen-EL-oh-pee], who was always faithful to Odysseus. For years she managed to put them off by telling them she had to finish weaving a funeral shroud for Odysseus's old father. She worked on it during the day and unwove it at night. She and her son were marking time, somehow believing that Odysseus would return—someday. As the years passed and Telemachus grew into a young man, he became more and more determined to make a journey of his own and look for his father. The goddess Athena [uh-THEEN-uh], for whom Odysseus was a special favorite, began to notice his son. Telemachus was a thoughtful and prudent young man. With proper guidance, he could do great things like his father. The goddess began to plan how to get them back together. But she was thwarted by another god, Poseidon [poh-SIE-don] of the sea, who hated the resourceful Odysseus as much as Athena admired and loved him.

Meanwhile, where was Odysseus, and what was he doing? Why, after ten years of war, was it going to take another ten years to get home again, back to his loved ones, faithful Penelope and thoughtful Telemachus?

The Wanderings of Odysseus

Poseidon

Odysseus began his long voyage to Ithaca after the conclusion of the Trojan War. On the way, he and his crew visited the land of the Lotus-eaters, where it seemed always a summer afternoon and where his men wished to stay forever. Eating the sweet fruit of the lotus made them forget past and future, kin and home, everything but the happy, drowsy, blissful present. Odysseus finally managed to drag them away from this paradise, and they traveled on to the island of the terrible one-eyed Cyclops [SI-klops], Polyphemus [paw-lee-FEE-muhs], son of his enemy Poseidon. Odysseus and his men escaped from Polyphemus by first blinding him and then riding and hanging on under the shaggy bellies of sheep as they fled the monster's cave. Then they visited Aeolus [EE-oh-luhs], lord of the winds, on his floating island, who gave them a fair wind to blow them home and all the other winds tied up in a bag. But some of the men were too

© Mark Twain Media, Inc., Publishers

102

curious and untied the bag, and the ship was driven back to Aeolus, who refused to help them again.

When they were finally underway again they sailed for many weeks without sighting land. Desperate to replenish their supplies of food and water, they stopped at the first island they came to. Odysseus and his sailors waded ashore, tired, hungry and dispirited, in search of fresh water. Odysseus climbed a hill for a bird's-eye view. He saw no people or houses, just a thin spiral of blue smoke from a distant clump of trees. Hoping it was a friendly hearth, he sent Eurylochus [yoo-RIL-oh-kuhs] with half the men to investigate while he and the rest of the crew stayed to guard the ship.

Led by the smoke, Eurylochus and his men came to a beautiful marble palace. But they were terrified to see wild animals roving about: lions, tigers, and wolves, though too drowsy and quiet to be dangerous. Recovering their courage, the men crept on to the palace. The animals did not jump at them, but lay down and tried to lick their hands, like good dogs. Eurylochus thought he saw a pleading look in their eyes, almost human, like the eyes of confused and troubled men. Patting their heads, he walked on to the main door of the palace. He heard music and singing. He called out, and a beautiful woman appeared. She seemed to be floating toward him, her dress and scarfs fluttering in the soft breeze. In a low, sweet voice, she invited him in.

But her eyes—small, glittering, and cruel—gave her away. As his men crowded into the hall, Eurylochus quietly backed away from the door. The beasts gathered around him and began to utter mournful cries.

Eurylochus crept up to a window and looked into the hall. A great banquet was going on—all kinds of hot food and luscious fruits and sweets. Eurylochus was extremely hungry. Had he been too cautious? He waited and watched his men finish their meal and stretch themselves, yawning; some were falling asleep in their chairs. Then their hostess took up a little ivory wand and lightly touched each one of them. What a change! Long ears began to grow out of their heads, their skins grew bristly, their noses turned to snouts, and their hands and feet to hoofs. They fell on all fours and began to waddle about, grunting. They had been turned into pigs!

Now Eurylochus knew that this lovely lady, with a voice so sweet and low, was Circe [SIR-see] the Enchantress. No wonder the lions and tigers had looked at him so sadly. They had been men, too.

Circe led the pigs out of the palace and shut them up in a filthy sty. Tossing them a bagful of acorns, she laughed at them as they crowded to the fence with pleading looks.

Eurylochus hurried back to the ship and told what had happened. Odysseus at once ran off to rescue his men, sword in hand. Suddenly, the god Hermes [HER-meez] appeared to him. "You are a brave man," Hermes said, "but you can't fight Circe's sorcery. Your sword is of no use against her magic." He gave Odysseus a green twig called moly. "Hang on to this; it will keep you safe from sorcery." Hermes disappeared, and Odysseus went on

Hermes

Hermes = Mercury

© Mark Twain Media, Inc., Publishers   103

to the palace. Circe met him, all smiles. The poor beasts crowded close, almost as though to warn him.

Circe seated him at the table and watched him eat. What a strong, handsome man he was! What a fine, large boar he would make!

But when she touched him with the wand, nothing happened! Odysseus did not go down on all fours or start grunting. No! He leaped at her with sword drawn, the moly in his left hand. "Witch!" he cried. "Release my friends!" She was so terrified that she knelt down and screamed for mercy. Yes! She would do anything he asked. She would free them all and then help them on their way.

Circe ran to the pig sties and touched all the boars, and they became men again. She did the same with the other animals. They rose up as men and stretched and talked with each other, no longer grunting and growling, but speaking as men do.

The enchantress, tamed by bold Odysseus, kept her word. She gave them water, wine, and food. She gave them new clothes and a new sail for their ship. When everything was ready, the men put on their new clothes and carried on board all the things Circe had provided: wine and water, barley meal and smoked meats. They grabbed their oars, the sail bellowed out with a favoring tail wind, and they were off again toward Ithaca and home.

Circe

Beyond the Myth

1. What kind of man is Odysseus? What are his chief qualities?

2. What is the main point of the story of Circe? Is there any special significance to the fact that she turns Odysseus's men into <u>pigs</u>?

Identify:

Penelope	Circe	Eurylochus
Telemachus	The Lotus-eaters	moly
Athena	Cyclops	Aeolus

Define:

sty   shroud

Locate on a map:

Ithaca

© Mark Twain Media, Inc., Publishers

Name _____ Date _____

The Odyssey: Part One

1. Penelope was the faithful _____ of Odysseus.

2. She kept the unwelcome suitors at bay by pretending to weave a funeral _____

for Odysseus's father.

3. Telemachus was the thoughtful, prudent _____ of Odysseus.

4. Among the gods, the special friend of Odysseus was _____ .

5. His particular enemy among the gods was _____ .

6. In their long voyage home they came to the land of the _____ ,

where people forgot time, and it seemed always to be a summer afternoon.

7. In another adventure they encountered a one-eyed monster called the _____ .

8. On a floating island they met Aeolus, lord of the _____ .

9. On Circe's isle, Odysseus sent his right-hand man, _____ , to spy out the

land.

10. When Odysseus went to rescue his men from Circe, he met the god Hermes, who gave him

a sprig of a plant called _____ to protect him from Circe's magic.

The Odyssey: Part Two

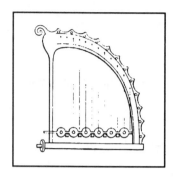

The Wanderings of Odysseus (*continued*)

Odysseus = Ulysses

After leaving Circe's [SIR-seez] isle, Odysseus [oh-DIS-see-uhs] and his men continued their voyage. They had been warned that they would have to sail past the island of the Sirens [SI-rens], whose sweet songs lured men to death. Odysseus knew what to do. As they approached the Sirens' isle, he cut a cake of wax into small bits with his sword and filled the ears of his men so that, laboring at the oars, they could not hear the Siren's song. His own ears, however, remained open. He had his men bind him to the mast, and they rowed on past the rocks where the white bones of dead men gleamed in the dark water. The Song of the Sirens rose sweet and clear:

> Come on, great Odysseus, slow down your ship. Listen! No one has ever passed this way without pausing to hear our honey-sweet voices. We know of you and your fame and glorious deeds. We know how the Trojans wrought and fought in the Great War. We know all the toils and triumphs of Mankind on the whole wide earth.

Odysseus trembled with desire to stay; he strained at his bonds. He begged his comrades to unbind him; they only bound him tighter and rowed faster till they were well beyond those delectable and deadly voices. Then they drew the wax from their ears and unbound their chief.

But now—a new danger! They had to pass through a narrow strait of water where on one side there was a man-eating monster with six heads named Scylla [SIL-luh] and on the other side a whirlpool called Charybdis [kuh-RIB-dis], which sucked in the waters and drew them down to the bottom of the sea, then spewed them up again to spatter against the rocky cliffs. In trying to escape one peril, they might fall to the other. Staring down in dread at the whirlpool, Charybdis, they were aware too late of the six heads and necks and mouths of Scylla approaching from the other side.

Odysseus and his men sailed past many dangers.

© Mark Twain Media, Inc., Publishers

She seized six of the crew, drew them up the cliff, and devoured them at the mouth of her cave. Odysseus saw them, heard their cries, and could do nothing to save them. It was the most pitiful sight, he said, he had ever seen in all his sufferings and journeyings.

Escaping these perils at the price of six comrades lost, they passed

to the Island of the Sun, where sleek cattle and fat sheep grazed. Circe had warned them to stay away from it, but Eurylochus [yoo-RIL-oh-kuhs] and the rest pleaded their exhaustion. One night would do no harm.

Odysseus argued against it, but finally consented on condition that no one touch the browsing flocks and herds. But while he slept, his men, who felt they were dying of hunger, slew and butchered some of the cattle and roasted the steaks for a good meal. The old Sun God, Helius [HEE-lee-uhs], was furious and complained to Zeus [ZOOS]. If atonement were not made, he said, he would put a spoke in the wheel of Apollo's [uh-PAW-lohz] chariot so that the sun would cease to shine. Zeus told him he would take care of the punishment of these cattle thieves.

The men feasted for six days and on the seventh sailed off. Suddenly, a cloud shut in around them, and a terrible storm arose. In the midst of this, Zeus hurled a thunderbolt, which hit the ship with such force that the rowers were thrown into the sea, drowning them all. Odysseus, alone, made a raft from the mast and part of the keel. As the ship sank, he took his seat on the raft and rowed hard with his hands.

For nine days he rode that raft, and on the tenth night the gods brought him to the isle of Ogygia. Here lived a beautiful sea nymph with braided hair, Calypso [kuh-LIP-soh] by name. She found him on the beach nearly dead and took pity on him. Reviving him, she led him to her home and nursed and cared for him. Soon her pity turned to love. She longed to have him for her lord and master, promising him that if he took her as his bride he would never grow old or die. He was grateful to Calypso, who had saved his life, and he stayed with her seven years. But eventually his longing for home became too strong. He yearned for Penelope [pen-EL-oh-pee] and Telemachus [teh-LEM-uh-kuhs] and the people of Ithaca. The day finally came when the fair goddess helped him to resume his journey.

Calypso loaned him tools to build a small ship and helped equip it.

> **As punishment for eating Helius's cattle, Zeus struck Odysseus's ship with a thunderbolt.**

Zeus = Jupiter, Jove

Apollo = Apollo

Calypso

Poseidon = Neptune

He sailed off toward the isle of Phaeacia, keeping the constellation of the Big Bear (Callisto) on his left as a guide, as Calypso had told him. Poseidon [poh-SIE-don], though, was still his bitter foe and out to get him. In a fury, the Sea God stirred up the waves with his three-pronged fishing spear, the trident. In this terrible storm, Odysseus went overboard, but he was saved by a sea nymph, Ino [I-noh], who threw him a magic veil that held him up like a life preserver until he could swim ashore. In this way he came to Phaeacia, unkempt, nearly naked, and almost dead.

Here on the beach he was found by Princess Nausicaä [noh-SIK-ee-uh], daughter of King Alcinous [al-SIN-oo-uhs], and her maidens. While her maids ran off shrieking with fright at the sight of a strange man, Nausicaä revived Odysseus with food and drink and gave him clothing. She told him exactly how to reach her father's palace, how to be discreet, where to go, and what to do. In the great room he would find her mother, the queen, weaving yarn dyed the color of the wine-purple sea, and her father, drinking wine like a god. She told him to kneel down as a suppliant, embrace her mother's knees, and make his plea for aid to reach his home. If he did that, she was sure all would be well.

Poseidon was Odysseus's bitter enemy and tried to keep him from returning to Ithaca.

Odysseus did as she advised and was received with great hospitality. King Alcinous hosted his guest with games and gifts and a great feast. Odysseus, though enjoying the supper and entertainment with a glad heart, had not yet told who he was; his hosts believed he was just a wayfarer trying to get home again. But when the bard (minstrel), old Demodocus [dee-MAWD-oh-kuhs], tuned his lyre and began to sing about the sack of Troy and the Wooden Horse, Odysseus was so overcome that he wept. King Alcinous, now suspicious that his guest was not just a commoner, politely suggested that he tell them his name. Odysseus could hold back no longer. He told his name, his home, and his travels and adventures since leaving Troy.

At the end of the last tale, Alcinous, much moved, could only say, simply but with utmost courtesy: "King Odysseus, be assured: we will send you home. That is a promise."

Identify:

The Sirens	Scylla	Charybdis
The Old Sun God	Calypso	Ino
Alcinous	Nausicaä	Demodocus

Define:

wayfarer   bard   lyre   suppliant

Name _____   Date _____

The Odyssey: Part Two

1. The sea nymphs whose deadly songs lured men to death were the _____ .

Odysseus escaped them by filling the ears of his men with _____ so that they could not

hear.

2. Passing through a narrow strait, the sailors encountered the double danger of the devouring six-

headed monster, _____ , on one side and the whirlpool, _____ , on the

other.

3. The cattle of the Pastures of the Sun were sacred to the old Sun God (before Apollo),

_____ .

4. The goddess who owned the island of Ogygia was the beautiful nymph, _____ ,

with whom Odysseus stayed for seven years.

5. When he finally left her, he guided himself, as she directed him to do, by the constellation of

Callisto, or the _____ _____ , on his left hand.

6. On his way to Phaeacia, his enemy, _____ , nearly drowned him, but he was saved

by the sea-nymph, _____ .

7. On the beach of Phaeacia, half dead, he was found by the royal princess, _____ .

8. She told him how to approach the queen, her mother, and her father, King _____ .

9. At the banquet he gave himself away by weeping when Demodocus, the _____ ,

sang of the Trojan War.

10. The king promised he would _____

_____ .

The Odyssey: Part Three

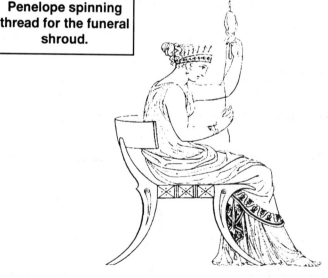

The Homecoming of Odysseus

Odysseus = Ulysses

As Odysseus [oh-DIS-see-uhs] was struggling against many dangers to get back to Ithaca, his son, Telemachus [teh-LEM-uh-kuhs], set out to find news of him. He traveled to Sparta, where King Menelaus [men-eh-LAY-uhs] told him he had heard that Odysseus was a lonely prisoner of the nymph, Calypso [ka-LIP-soh]. Saddened by this news, Telemachus began his own journey back to Ithaca.

Meanwhile, King Alcinous [al-SIN-oo-uhs], true to his word, sent Odysseus back to Ithaca in one of the Phaecian ships. When they reached the shore of his native land, the crew laid him, sleeping, on the beach and left him. When he awoke, Athena appeared to him. She told him that he was home at last, and then explained the dangerous situation at his house. His wife's suitors were eating them out of house and home. The bully of the suitors, Antinous [an-TIN-oo-uhs], had found out that Penelope [pen-EL-oh-pee] had tricked them with the never-finished shroud, so now Penelope had no more excuses; she would be forced to choose a new husband.

If any of the suitors recognized him, Odysseus's life would be in danger. So Athena disguised him as an old beggar and sent him to stay with Eumaeus [you-MAY-uhs], the swineherd, until he could formulate a plan for dealing with the vile suitors.

Athena = Minerva

Penelope spinning thread for the funeral shroud.

In a few days, Telemachus returned, and Athena [uh-THEEN-uh], for a time, restored his father to his usual form so that the son would recognize him. After the joyful reunion, Odysseus and Telemachus together began to lay plans for giving the suitors what they deserved. They decided not to let Penelope know that Odysseus had returned—she had almost given up hope that her dear husband would ever come home again.

Once their plans were made, the men wasted no time in putting them into action. Telemachus went ahead to the palace to prepare the way, and his father, disguised as an old man, followed with Eumaeus. Near the door of the outer court lay an old dog, Argus [AR-guhs], whom Odysseus had raised as a pup years ago. Odysseus had left for Troy before the dog was fully grown. Now, as Odysseus drew near, the old dog knew him and feebly wagged his tail. Looking his last upon his

© Mark Twain Media, Inc., Publishers

loving master, he dropped his head and died. Faithful Argus had waited for his master twenty years.

Greeted at the door by Telemachus, they entered the hall. Odysseus, a beggar in his own house, had to endure many humiliations. A few of the suitors were kind and gave the old man bread, but most were indifferent. Antinous, the bully, contemptuously threw a footstool at the beggar, striking his shoulder. Unfaithful servants, their discipline gone lax over the years, insulted him. This lack of courtesy and respect for a supplant guest violated one of the basic rules of ancient Greek life, but the fated avenger put up with it for a time.

As the days passed, Penelope, who never dreamed her husband was home, reluctantly decided that Odysseus was surely dead and she had no alternative but to choose another husband. She sent word that, to finally settle the matter, she would give herself to whoever could bend the great bow of Odysseus. Odysseus, disguised in rags, claimed the right to try too, though the suitors laughed and jeered. Eumaeus placed the bow in Odysseus's hands. Then he went to the housekeeper, old Eurycleia [yoo-ree-KLEE-uh], and told her to shut all the inner doors and keep the women and servants inside, whatever happened. A loyal ox-herd, Philoitios [phil-OY-tee-ohs], whom Odyssesus had taken into his confidence, went forth and barred the outer gates, tying them with ropes. He then came back and stood by. To fight the wicked suitors—and there were many of them—were just four men: Odysseus, Telemachus, Eumaeus, and Philoitios.

As Athena restored him to his usual form, Odysseus bent the bow easily and twanged the bowstring. The sound was like a challenge to arms; the suitors grew pale. From the sky burst a thunderpeal, the "drum" of Zeus [ZOOS]. The High God was weighing all in the balance.

Odysseus notched an arrow to the bow and drew the string back to his shoulder. The arrow flew straight to the mark, through the holes of twelve axes, one behind the other, and into the wall behind.

The suitors were amazed and afraid, but they had no warning of what was to come. They tried to go on with the feast, but Odysseus let fly with the bow and arrows and killed all the suitors.

It was not a fight, but a massacre. Yet the slaughter of the suitors was not undeserved. They had been wasting the substance of that household for years, they had harassed and insulted the lady of that house and her

Odysseus proved his worth by drawing his bow and shooting an arrow through twelve axes.

Zeus = Jupiter, Jove

Zeus

© Mark Twain Media, Inc., Publishers

111

son, and they had broken heaven's laws designed to protect the poor, the weak, and the stranger. Odysseus had a personal feud with these men, but he was also an agent of Divine Justice.

When the terrible fight was over, Odysseus made himself known to his wife. At first Penelope could not believe it was truly Odysseus standing before her. After twenty years, faithful, long-suffering wife that she was, she demanded proof. Odysseus told her how he had built their bed out of a living olive tree in the courtyard and built up their bedroom around that tree. Only the two of them knew this. Then Penelope believed and ran to embrace and kiss him. They held each other closely and wept with joy.

That night, their good angel, Athena, held back the dawn and the Horses of the Sun to make longer their first night of reunion and happiness.

Odysseus and Penelope Reunited

Beyond the Myth

From an overall moral point of view, do you think the suitors deserved their fate?

Identify:

Antinous	Argus	Eumaeus
Philoitios	Eurycleia	

Define:

suppliant	lax
swineherd	ox-herd

Locate on a map:

Sparta	Ithaca

© Mark Twain Media, Inc., Publishers

Name_____ Date _____

The Odyssey: Part Three

1. Antinous was the _____ of the suitors.

2. Seeking news of his father, Telemachus visited King Menelaus at _____ .

3. To hide his identity, Athena disguised Odysseus to look like an old _____ .

4. As Odysseus, Telemachus, and Eumaeus approached the palace, Odysseus encountered

dying _____ , his faithful dog.

5. Penelope said she would give herself to whoever could bend Odysseus's _____ .

6. Odysseus shot an arrow through the holes of _____ _____ , one

behind the other.

7. Odysseus revealed himself to Penelope and proved his identity by noting how he had built

their bed out of an _____ _____ in the courtyard.

8. That night Athena, to increase their happiness, made the _____ come later.

Name_____ Date _____

THE ODYSSEY CROSSWORD

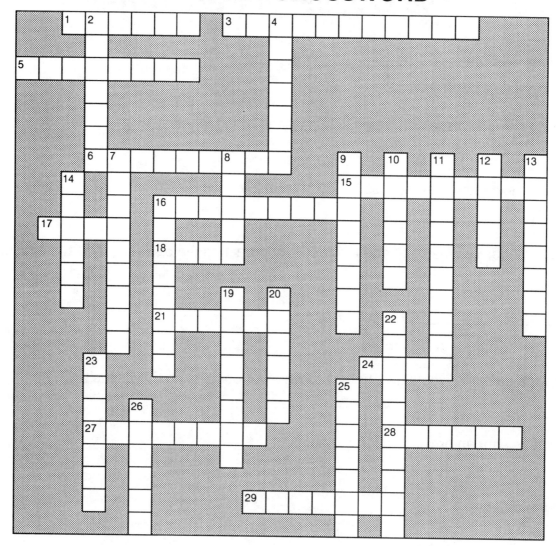

ACROSS
1. What Penelope was weaving
3. Zeus destroyed the ship with it
5. She rescued Odysseus on the beach at Phaeacia
6. The old bard
15. Odysseus's bed was made from it (two words)
16. The whirlpool
17. Magical green twig
18. Musical instrument that the minstrel played
21. Six-headed monster
24. What Circe turned the men into
27. Bully suitor
28. Odysseus's home
29. Beautiful sea nymph; Odysseus stayed with her for seven years

DOWN
2. The suitors wanted to be Penelope's _____
4. Odysseus's Roman name
7. The housekeeper
8. The sorceress
9. Odysseus's enemy
10. Their songs lured men to their death
11. Odysseus's son
12. Faithful dog
13. Odysseus's wife
14. Lord of the winds
16. The Big Bear constellation
19. King of Phaeacia
20. What the men killed on the Island of the Sun
22. Loyal ox-herd who helped in the fight
23. The swineherd
25. One-eyed monster
26. Goddess who was fond of Odysseus

© Mark Twain Media, Inc., Publishers

The Beginning of Rome

The epic of Rome is the *Aeneid* of Virgil, the greatest poem in the Latin language. Virgil modeled it on the *Iliad* and the *Odyssey*. He tried to connect the origins of Rome to events that followed the fiery destruction of Troy by the Greeks. From about the 200s B.C., the Romans tried to relate the origins of their gods to the Greek myths. As things turned out, most Roman mythology simply became Greek mythology dressed up with Latin names.

The Roman Venus [VEE-nuhs], who watched over the fertility and flourishing of gardens, assumed identification with Aphrodite [af-roh-DIE-tee]. Through her son, the Trojan prince Aeneas [ee-NEE-uhs], she came to have a unique role in the stories the Romans developed to connect their origins with the Greek heroic age.

Venus

Aeneas Finds a New Land

As the Greeks burned and conquered the city of Troy, very few of Troy's citizens escaped. Among those that did was Aeneas, a prince. He, his father, and his son fled to the hills where they gathered with other refugees. Aeneas's wife, Creusa [kree-OO-suh], was killed in the mad rush out of the city, but her spirit came to Aeneas and told him that he was

destined to find a new home in Italy, and that his descendants would build a beautiful city and empire that would rule the entire world.

Aeneas led the Trojan refugees to the new land, encountering many difficulties along the way. They built a town on the banks of the Tiber River. In time, his son, Ascanius [as-KAN-ee-uhs], grew up and moved to another town, Alba Longa. It was here that the descendants of Aeneas and Ascanius, the twins Romulus [ROM-yoo-luhs] and Remus [REE-muhs], were born.

> **Romulus and Remus were found and cared for by a mother wolf when they were babies.**

Romulus and Remus and the Dream of Rome

The ancient Romans believed that Romulus and Remus were born of a mortal mother and the war god, Mars [MARZ]. The best-known version

Mars = Ares

of this legend tells of an evil king of Alba Longa who had deposed his brother, the rightful king, killed this king's sons, and forced their sister, Rhea Sylvia [REE-uh SIL-vee-uh], to become a priestess to keep her from having sons. But Rhea Sylvia was loved by Mars, the War God, who made her his bride, and she gave birth to twin sons, Romulus and Remus.

Rhea Sylvia died when the twins were still babies. Since no one else cared for them, their wicked uncle had them placed in a watertight basket and set them drifting down the Tiber.

Nature was kind to the little fellows. The winds were not too rough, and the sun warmed them. The basket-boat rocked gently like a cradle, or a mother's warm and loving arms. But there was one thing they lacked—milk. Being healthy boy babies, they were soon very hungry.

Mars, the god of war, was the father of Romulus and Remus.

Father Tiber [TIE-ber], the river god, helped them. He called in all the little feeder streams to empty their waters into his. When the Tiber overflowed his banks, the basket floated up high onto the sands; then the waters drew back.

A mother wolf came prowling along. (The wolf was an animal sacred to Mars.) Seeing the basket, she trotted over and saw the babies sucking their fingers; she heard them wailing with hunger. Poor famished mites! These little human children reminded the mother wolf of her own cubs, who could already stand on their feet, though of course they had four instead of only two. The mother wolf caressed these furless infants with her tongue. Never did she think of eating them! With her paw she rolled them, one by one, out of the basket and over the level ground to her cave. She dragged them inside and put them in the downy nest with her own babies. When the little wolves woke up and drank their mother's milk, Romulus and Remus drank too.

For some time they lived in the cave and played with the cubs, rolling around and wrestling with them. In this way they grew fast and strong. They could walk long before most human babies could. They thrived on wolf's milk.

One day when the mother wolf was away, they toddled to the mouth of the cave and saw the sun and the sky. A shepherd passing by saw them creep out and start to play on the grass. He was a kind man and took them home. He and his wife raised them as their own children. They learned to drink their milk from cups and to wear the little shirts, or tunics, that their new mother made for them. They loved these new parents, but never forgot their

© Mark Twain Media, Inc., Publishers

wolf mother. Often they ran back to the cave to see her and play and wrestle and dance with the cubs. The little wolves were their first playmates, their foster brothers and sisters.

They loved the river and waded and swam in it and made sand castles along the shore. One day Romulus said that when he grew up he would build a house beside the Tiber, with many rooms, all of marble, and with wide porches and high columns. His brother, Remus, did not live to grow up. But Romulus in time drove out his wicked uncle from Alba Longa and built his dream house on the banks of the Tiber where the mother wolf had nursed him and his twin. Friends came and built their houses around his. In this way a mighty city was founded, with Romulus, for whom it was named, as first king (supposedly in 753 B.C.). This was the beginning of the long glories of majestic Rome.

Beyond the Myth

1. Explain how the Greek gods were "taken over" by the Romans.

2. Using a map of our solar system, locate the following planets: Jupiter, Saturn, Neptune, Mercury, and Venus. You already know where their names come from. Now locate Mars, Uranus, Pluto, and Earth. What are the origins of these names?

3. Using resources in your library, can you find other stories about humans being raised by wild animals?

Identify:
   Virgil   Aeneas   Creusa   Ascanius   Rhea Sylvia

Define:
   epic   Latin   descendants

Locate on a map:
   Italy   Tiber River   Alba Longa   Rome

Name _____ Date _____

The Beginning of Rome

1. A long narrative poem telling of the origins and ideals of a nation and relating the deeds of a

national hero is called an _____ .

2. The author of the *Aeneid* is _____ .

3. The Greek goddess Aphrodite became the Roman goddess _____ . She was the

mother of _____ , who escaped from Troy.

4. The mother of Romulus and Remus was _____ _____ .

Their father was _____ , the god of _____ .

5. The twins were born in the town of _____ _____ .

6. When the twins were set adrift in the basket, they were saved by the river god, Father

_____ , who called in other rivers to float the basket to shore.

7. The mother wolf took the infants to her_____ . They drank her _____

along with her own cubs.

8. The year 753 B.C. is the mythical symbolic date for the founding of the city of _____ .

© Mark Twain Media, Inc., Publishers   118

Name _____ Date _____

MYTH MAKING

Here's your opportunity to write a myth of your own! You may use any of the classical characters from Greek or Roman mythology that you've learned about, or you may invent your own, but you should tell about how something came to be or why something is the way it is. Your story may be set in ancient times, the not-so-distant past, the present, or the future. Be creative! Be sure to write neatly and watch your spelling, grammar, and punctuation. Use more paper if you need to.

Title _____

_____

_____

_____

_____

_____

_____

_____

_____

_____

_____

_____

_____

_____

_____

_____

_____

© Mark Twain Media, Inc., Publishers   119

Name _____ Date _____

STAR ATTRACTIONS

Many constellations get their names from characters in mythology or from nature. Using the star chart on page 121 and other sources about constellations, can you identify these constellations?

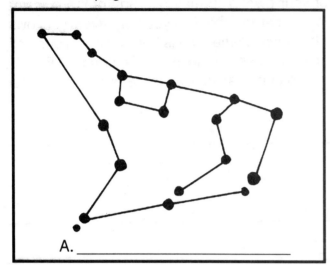

A. _____

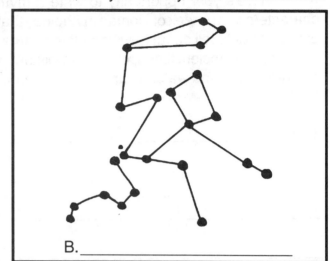

B. _____

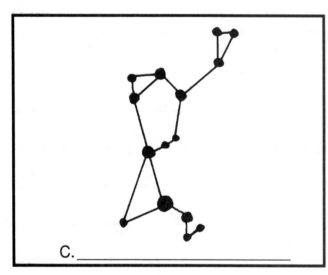

C. _____

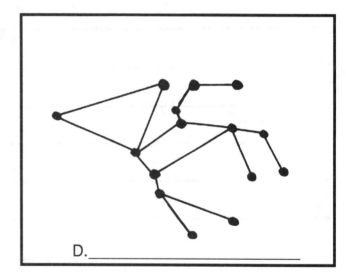

D. _____

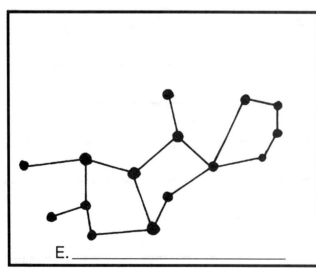

E. _____

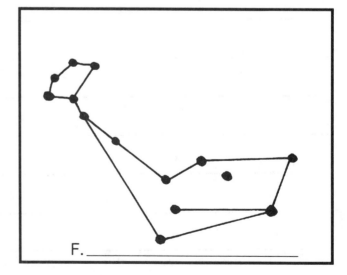

F. _____

© Mark Twain Media, Inc., Publishers

STAR CHART

The chart below shows some of the most common constellations. This is the position of the constellations from October 1 through December 16 in the northern hemisphere. How many of these can you find in the night sky?

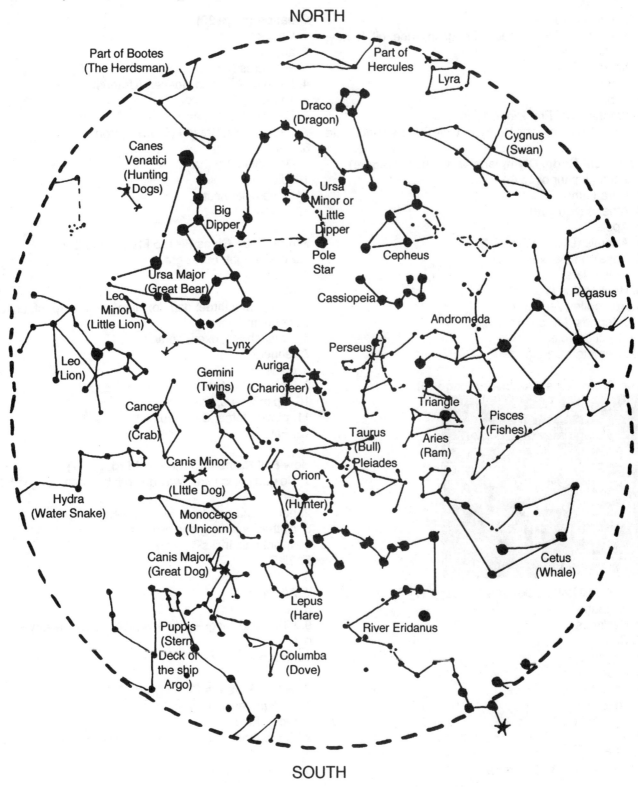

NORTH

Part of Bootes
(The Herdsman)

Part of Hercules

Lyra

Draco
(Dragon)

Cygnus
(Swan)

Canes
Venatici
(Hunting
Dogs)

Ursa
Minor or
Little
Dipper

Big
Dipper

Pole
Star

Cepheus

Pegasus

Ursa Major
(Great Bear)

Leo
Minor
(Little Lion)

Cassiopeia

Andromeda

Lynx

Perseus

Leo
(Lion)

Gemini
(Twins)

Auriga
(Charioteer)

Triangle

Pisces
(Fishes)

Cancer
(Crab)

Taurus
(Bull)

Aries
(Ram)

Canis Minor
(Little Dog)

Pleiades

Orion
(Hunter)

Hydra
(Water Snake)

Monoceros
(Unicorn)

Cetus
(Whale)

Canis Major
(Great Dog)

Lepus
(Hare)

River Eridanus

Puppis
(Stern
Deck of
the ship
Argo)

Columba
(Dove)

SOUTH

© Mark Twain Media, Inc., Publishers

Answers to Quizzes

What is a Myth? (page 3)
1. values
2. Indians, Egyptians, Greeks, Romans
3. religious
4. magic, crops
5. Accept any four: speech, fire, grain, wine, oil, honey, agriculture, metal work
6. horses
7. behavior
8. hubris
9. Washington, Franklin, Lincoln
10. Paul Bunyan, John Henry, or Little Engine That Could

The Great Gods, Olympians and Others (page 9)
1. Zeus (Jupiter or Jove)
2. Hera (Juno)
3. Athena (Minerva)
4. Apollo
5. Artemis (Diana, "Cynthia")
6. Poseidon (Neptune)
7. Ares (Mars)
8. Hephaestus (Vulcan)
9. Aphrodite (Venus)
10. Hermes (Mercury)
11. Hestia (Vesta)
12. Demeter (Ceres)

The Great Gods Crossword (page 10)

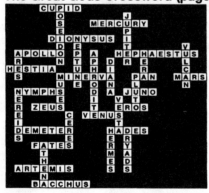

Greek and Italian Geography (page 17)
1. Aegean
2. Cyclades
3. Corinth
4. Olympus
5. ruler
6. barley, grapes, olives
7. seacoasts
8. Tyrrhenian; Adriatic
9. Po
10. Tiber
11. Sicily, Sardinia, Corsica

12. Appenines; Alps
13. wheat, grapes, olives; sheep
14. Naples

Creation (page 20)
1. Chaos
2. abyss
3. egg; Eros (Love)
4. Earth (Gaea) and Heaven (Uranus)
5. Titans
6. Cronos; Golden Age
7. Zeus; Silver, Brazen (Bronze), Iron
8. flood
9. Deucalion, Pyrrha
10. died
11. ambrosia, nectar
12. image

Prometheus Gives Fire to Man (page 24)
1. Forethought, Foresight
2. Titans
3. clay
4. Accept any three: dog, fox, lion, deer, serpent, dove
5. stone and bone
6. dogs, sheep, oxen, horses
7. fennel
8. colder
9. blacksmith, Aetna
10. Epimetheus, box
11. power, force, Caucasus
12. Fate

How Evil Came Into the World (page 27)
1. No god could take away any gift that another god had given.
2. honey and gall, love and hate, etc.
3. clothes, spinning and sewing
4. sweet talk, tricks
5. All-Gifted
6. sealed box
7. Afterthought
8. curiosity
9. All the bad things—sins and plagues and misery—flew out.
10. Hope

How the Seasons Came (page 31)
1. daylight, eyes, flowers, dizzy
2. Sicily, Eros
3. Persephone, Demeter, grain; Underworld
4. Eleusis
5. Celeus, temple

© Mark Twain Media, Inc., Publishers

6. famine
7. Iris, Hermes, Rhea
8. pomegranate seeds
9. Demeter, Hades
10. seed wheat

The Horses of the Sun (page 35)
1. Helius
2. "shining" or "shiner"
3. Horses of the Sun
4. Dawn
5. Taurus
6. Crab
7. Lion
8. Scorpio
9. middle way
10. Chaos
11. lightning bolt
12. poplar trees, amber

Glorious Apollo (page 39)
1. Delos
2. Leto and Zeus
3. ambrosia, nectar
4. frogs
5. dolphins
6. music, poetry
7. Parnassus
8. Delphic oracle
9. Crete
10. Pan
11. swans
12. Helius

White Goddess of the Moon (page 42)
1. matriarchal
2. Hyperion
3. Thea
4. Eos, Helius, Selene
5. silver, white horses
6. brown, "Little She-Bears"
7. night
8. animals
9. Leto, Zeus; Apollo
10. moon

Star Myth (page 45)
1. Callisto
2. Arcas
3. Zeus's, Hera
4. bear
5. Callisto
6. shepherd
7. Zeus

8. bear
9. constellations
10. Poseidon
11. Pole
12. "Dippers" (Big and Little)

Love and the Soul (page 50)
1. "Soul"
2. Cupid
3. Venus (Aphrodite)
4. West Wind
5. sisters
6. oil, lamp
7. trust
8. grain; ants
9. wool
10. Styx; eagle
11. beauty
12. goddess

King Midas and the Golden Touch (page 54)
1. Silenus
2. Phrygia
3. gold
4. dog
5. food
6. daughter, Marigold
7. Pan
8. good natured
9. Pactolus, wash
10. anemones

Narcissus and Echo (page 57)
1. Diana (Artemis)
2. Juno (Hera)
3. last, first
4. narcissistic
5. echo
6. caves
7. Nemesis
8. himself
9. Styx
10. flower

The First Aviators (page 60)
1. architect, builder, inventor
2. Minos, Labyrinth
3. Theseus, Ariadne
4. thread
5. birds
6. reeds, feathers, wax
7. Crete
8. sun, feathers
9. Icarian
10. Apollo

© Mark Twain Media, Inc., Publishers

The Youth of Hercules (page 64)

1. Alcmena; Zeus
2. demigod
3. Thebes
4. prophet
5. snakes; lion
6. Pleasure, Vice; Virtue
7. Virtue
8. his music teacher
9. Megara
10. Hera
11. Delphic oracle
12. Twelve Labors

The Twelve Labors of Hercules: Part One (page 68)

1. Eurystheus
2. lion
3. He wrestled with it, then strangled it.
4. Hydra, heads
5. Iolaus; cauterizing
6. crab
7. deer
8. Artemis
9. boar, Centaurs
10. chasing it in the snow; it died of exhaustion

The Twelve Labors of Hercules: Part Two (page 71)

1. Augean Stables
2. rivers
3. one tenth
4. Olympic games
5. birds
6. rattle
7. Crete
8. Minos
9. Wild Mares of Diomedes
10. He and his men captured Diomedes.

The Twelve Labors of Hercules: Part Three (page 75)

1. belt, Amazons
2. captive
3. Europe, Asia (men, women)
4. cattle
5. Pillars of Hercules, Gibraltar
6. Golden Apples
7. Prometheus
8. Zeus
9. Atlas, apples, sky
10. dog

Hercules Crossword (page 76)

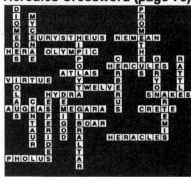

Perseus and Medusa (page 80)

1. Danaë
2. gold
3. chest
4. Dictys; king
5. shield, helmet, sandals
6. Ukraine; Gray Sisters
7. North Wind
8. shield
9. invisible
10. Pegasus

Perseus and Andromeda (page 84)

1. Atlas; stone
2. Abyssinia (Ethiopia); Andromeda, Cepheus, Cassiopeia
3. Nereids
4. scales
5. Medusa's
6. stone
7. Argos
8. discus
9. Athena; aegis
10. constellations

Bellerophon and Pegasus (page 87)

1. Pegasus
2. Athena; bit and bridle
3. Proetus; Anteia
4. hospitality
5. Iobates, Lycia
6. Zeus
7. lion, goat, snake
8. weapon
9. hubris; Mount Olympus
10. thunder, lightning

The Trojan War: Part One (page 90)

1. Homer
2. Black Sea
3. discord, quarreling
4. Hera, Athena, Aphrodite
5. Paris, Priam

© Mark Twain Media, Inc., Publishers

6. Kingly power, wisdom and glory in war, the most beautiful woman in the world
7. Aphrodite
8. Helen
9. Menelaus
10. Aphrodite
11. host, guest
12. Agamemnon

The Trojan War: Part Two (page 93)

1. Achilles
2. Hector
3. Hector
4. Antilochus
5. Thetis
6. death
7. Hephaestus
8. Pleides, Orion, Big Bear

The Trojan War: Part Three (page 96)

1. Ares, Hera, Artemis
2. Scaean
3. Priam, Hecuba
4. neck
5. body
6. Iris, suppliant
7. funeral
8. nine
9. pyre, urn
10. urn, stones

The Trojan War: Part Four (page 100)

1. River Styx
2. heel
3. Paris
4. wooden horse
5. sailing for home
6. Sinon
7. Athena
8. Odysseus
9. Aeneas
10. Menelaus, Helen, Aphrodite

The Trojan War Crossword (page 101)

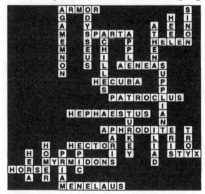

The Odyssey: Part One (page 105)

1. wife
2. shroud
3. son
4. Athena
5. Poseidon
6. Lotus Eaters
7. Cyclops
8. winds
9. Eurylochus
10. moly

The Odyssey: Part Two (page 109)

1. Sirens; wax
2. Scylla, Charybdis
3. Helius
4. Calypso
5. Big Bear or Big Dipper
6. Poseidon, Ino
7. Nausicaä
8. Alcinous
9. bard or minstrel
10. send Odysseus home

The Odyssey: Part Three (page 113)

1. bully
2. Sparta
3. beggar
5. bow
6. twelve axes
7. olive tree
8. dawn

The Odyssey Crossword (page 114)

The Beginning of Rome (page 118)

1. epic
2. Virgil
3. Venus; Aeneas
4. Rhea Sylvia; Mars, war
5. Alba Longa
6. Tiber
7. cave; milk
8. Rome

© Mark Twain Media, Inc., Publishers

Further Reading

For Young Readers:

Avery, Catherine B. (ed.) *The New Century Handbook of Greek Mythology and Legend.*
Brooks, Edward. *The Story of the Aeneid.*
Brooks, Edward. *The Story of the Iliad.*
Brooks, Edward. *The Story of the Odyssey.*
Hamilton, Edith. *Mythology.*
Hawthorne, Nathaniel. *Tanglewood Tales.*
Hutchinson, W.M.L. "Prometheus the Firebringer." *New Junior Classics, Vol. III.*
Kingsley, Charles. *The Heroes.*
Price, Margaret Evans. *Myths and Enchantment Tales.*
Rouse, W.H.D. *Gods, Heroes and Men.*
Tennyson, Alfred. "Ulysses."

For Older Readers and Teachers:

Aeschylus. *Prometheus Bound.*
Drinkwater, John. *Outline of Literature, Volume I.*
Frazer, Sir James George. *The Golden Bough.*
Graves, Robert. *The Greek Myths.*
Hesiod. *Theogony.*
Kazantzakis, Nikos. *The Odyssey: A Modern Sequel.* (Kimon Friar, translator)
Lattimore, Richard (translator). *The Iliad of Homer.*
Lattimore, Richard (translator). *The Odyssey of Homer.*
Oates, Whitney J. and Eugene O'Neill, Jr. *The Complete Greek Drama, Volume One.*
Ovid. *The Metamorphoses.*
Virgil. Dryden (translator). *The Aeneid.*

Answers to *Star Attractions* (page 120):
A. Ursa Major (Great Bear)
B. Hercules
C. Bootes (Herdsman)
D. Pegasus
E. Virgo (Virgin, Maiden)
F. Cetus (Whale)